A Woman's
Book 4
Impact on Her World

*Unlimited!...*Bible Studies for Today's Pentecostal Woman

*Arlene Allen, Peggy Musgrove,
Lori O'Dea, & Candy Tolbert*

GPH
Gospel Publishing House
Springfield, Missouri
02-0278

CONTENTS

FOREWORD

A Woman's Impact on Her World equips a woman to steward her influence wisely for the greatest good of Christ's kingdom by preparing her to respond to contemporary issues like pornography and the occult. It readies her to recognize the subtle pressures of materialism and secularism. And it equips her to make God-honoring choices in her sexual ethics and personal modesty. The authors' method is to focus each lesson on a contemporary issue, engage the topic by studying a related biblical passage, and illustrate the theme with a story of a woman in the Bible. They also facilitate interaction and application with questions for group discussion and personal reflection.

Today's Christian woman has the potential for tremendous impact on her world through her relationships and her integrity.

Who does she touch with her relationships? A woman's most profound potential for impact is on her family, with whom she has the most contact hours through the longest span of years. The second greatest potential for impact for some women is among coworkers or fellow students. A woman also has an impact on friends with whom she socializes in clubs, organizations, sports, or hobbies. Finally, a woman can have an impact on acquaintances—those in her neighborhood and community whom she lives near, buys from, or banks with. These relational networks are spheres of a woman's influence in her world. And for a Christian woman, they are potential fields for spiritual sowing and harvest.

And what of a woman's integrity? Her life is the light reflecting Jesus in a dark world. How can she grow in the true character of Christ while living in a contemporary culture that contradicts it? That's the purpose of this Bible studies series!

I encourage you to deliver the greatest possible impact to your world! Integrity is the cargo and relationships the conduit. Internalize Christ's example and incarnate Him through yours. Study these lessons on your own but don't stop there. Invite others to study with you. Community is the biggest draw for the contemporary person to Christ.

Deborah Gill
National Director, Christian Education
Commissioner of Discipleship
General Council of the Assemblies of God

PREFACE

This series of Bible studies was written in response to women and pastors across the United States who have asked for Pentecostal studies to use in their churches for group or individual study.

A Woman's Impact on Her World is a Pentecostal study written by Pentecostal women. This study is unique to any you have used before because the Pentecostal perspective is written into each lesson. The student will not have to search for the Pentecostal viewpoint—she needs only to embrace it and ask Jesus to help her apply it.

The Bible describes two types of relationships: vertical and horizontal. Our primary relationship is with God—all other relationships flow from it. In the Scriptures, relational problems increased as fast as the earth's population did. Adam and Eve refused to accept responsibility for their sin, thus hurting their relationship with God; Cain murdered his brother, Abel, in a fit of rage; Sarah mistreated her slave, Hagar; Jacob stole Esau's birthright; Laban cheated Jacob; and Joseph's brothers sold him into slavery. These are just a few examples of flawed relationships from the first book of the Bible.

These lessons will help you build right relationships, and learn the importance of restoring broken relationships. Within healthy relationships, we receive support, encouragement, acceptance, help, and love. However, in a bad relationship, we can experience rejection, judgment, discouragement, insensitivity, and jealousy.

Our prayer is that these studies will help you rejoice in your healthy relationships and examine your flawed relationships, giving you a renewed determination to heal them.

Arlene Allen
Director, Women's Ministries Department
General Council of the Assemblies of God

Her Personal Empowerment

CATCHING SIGHT

Introduction

*H*AVE IT YOUR way."

"Do yourself a favor."

"You owe it to yourself."

"You deserve a break today."

The world constantly promotes the "me first" philosophy in subtle—and overt—ways. Let's admit it, ours is an age of gross selfishness. We make every effort to look out for number one.

Leonard Bernstein, the famous orchestra conductor, performed one evening on television. During an informal time of discussion on the program, one admirer asked, "Mr. Bernstein, what is the most difficult instrument to play?"

He responded with quick wit, "Second fiddle. I can get plenty of first violinists, but to find one who plays second violin with as much enthusiasm, now that's a problem. And yet if no one plays second, we have no harmony."

How true! People have been selfish and individualistic since that moment Adam and Eve desired to become equal to God.

Jesus Christ offers a different way of living. While on earth, not only did He encourage humility, but He modeled it continually. Jesus challenged society's norms. To Him, greatness comes from serving—giving of yourself to God and others.

GETTING FOCUSED
Begin your study by considering the following:

What are some of the ways you are a selfish person?

BIBLE READING
Acts 1:1–8; 2:1–4,42–47

New International Version

1:1 In my former book, Theophilus, I wrote about all that Jesus began to do and to teach 2 until the day he was taken up to heaven, after giving instructions through the Holy Spirit to the apostles he had chosen. 3 After his suffering, he showed himself to these men and gave many convincing proofs that he was alive. He appeared to them over a period of forty days and spoke about the kingdom of God. 4 On one occasion, while he was eating with them, he gave them this command: "Do not leave Jerusalem, but wait for the gift my Father promised, which you have heard me speak about. 5 For John baptized with water, but in a few days you will be baptized with the Holy Spirit."

6 So when they met together, they asked him, "Lord, are you at this time going to restore the kingdom to Israel?"

7 He said to them: "It is not for you to know the times or dates the Father has set by his own authority. 8 But you will receive power when the Holy Spirit comes on you; and you will be my witnesses in

New Living Translation

1:1 Dear Theophilus: In my first book I told you about everything Jesus began to do and teach 2 until the day he ascended to heaven after giving his chosen apostles further instructions from the Holy Spirit. 3 During the forty days after his crucifixion, he appeared to the apostles from time to time and proved to them in many ways that he was actually alive. On these occasions he talked to them about the Kingdom of God.

4 In one of these meetings as he was eating a meal with them, he told them, "Do not leave Jerusalem until the Father sends you what he promised. Remember, I have told you about this before. 5 John baptized with water, but in just a few days you will be baptized with the Holy Spirit."

6 When the apostles were with Jesus, they kept asking him, "Lord, are you going to free Israel now and restore our kingdom?"

7 "The Father sets those dates," he replied, "and they are not for you to know. 8 But when the Holy Spirit has come upon you, you will receive power and will tell people about

New International Version

Jerusalem, and in all Judea and Samaria, and to the ends of the earth."

2:1 When the day of Pentecost came, they were all together in one place. 2 Suddenly a sound like the blowing of a violent wind came from heaven and filled the whole house where they were sitting. 3 They saw what seemed to be tongues of fire that separated and came to rest on each of them. 4 All of them were filled with the Holy Spirit and began to speak in other tongues as the Spirit enabled them.

42 They devoted themselves to the apostles' teaching and to the fellowship, to the breaking of bread and to prayer. 43 Everyone was filled with awe, and many wonders and miraculous signs were done by the apostles. 44 All the believers were together and had everything in common. 45 Selling their possessions and goods, they gave to anyone as he had need. 46 Every day they continued to meet together in the temple courts. They broke bread in their homes and ate together with glad and sincere hearts, 47 praising God and enjoying the favor of all the people. And the Lord added to their number daily those who were being saved.

New Living Translation

me everywhere—in Jerusalem, throughout Judea, in Samaria, and to the ends of the earth."

2:1 On the day of Pentecost, seven weeks after Jesus' resurrection, the believers were meeting together in one place. 2 Suddenly, there was a sound from heaven like the roaring of a mighty windstorm in the skies above them, and it filled the house where they were meeting. 3 Then, what looked like flames or tongues of fire appeared and settled on each of them. 4 And everyone present was filled with the Holy Spirit and began speaking in other languages, as the Holy Spirit gave them this ability.

42 They joined with the other believers and devoted themselves to the apostles' teaching and fellowship, sharing in the Lord's Supper and in prayer.

43 A deep sense of awe came over them all, and the apostles performed many miraculous signs and wonders. 44 And all the believers met together constantly and shared everything they had. 45 They sold their possessions and shared the proceeds with those in need. 46 They worshiped together at the Temple each day, met in homes for the Lord's Supper, and shared their meals with great joy and generosity—47 all the while praising God and enjoying the goodwill of all the people. And each day the Lord added to their group those who were being saved.

GAINING BIBLICAL INSIGHT
Depending on the Spirit

For days, the disciples had been on an emotional roller coaster. The dark agony of the Crucifixion was fresh in their memory. The subsequent time of seclusion was filled with fears for the future, until the women interrupted them with startling news of the empty tomb. Next they felt the overwhelming joy of seeing Jesus in person. Now, they had seen Him enough times to be fully convinced He was alive.

During these mystifying days, whenever Jesus presented himself, He continually talked of His Kingdom (Acts 1:3). Perplexed, the disciples wondered what His Kingdom would be like. Could He establish a Kingdom powerful enough to impact the mighty Roman Empire? The disciples would soon learn that Jesus' Kingdom was not political, but spiritual. It would not only affect Rome, but the entire world. It would come about not in courts or palaces through the power of personalities, but in the hearts of individual believers filled with the power of God.

The Disciples Anticipate the Coming Kingdom

Discussions of the Kingdom were not new to the disciples. Jesus had talked about His Kingdom from His earliest days of ministry on the mountains in Galilee (Matthew 5). Even on the night of His betrayal, the disciples had discussed the Kingdom privately among themselves (Luke 22:24-26).

How was the disciples' view of the Kingdom different from Jesus' view?

When the disciples tried to figure out who would have the most important position in the Kingdom, Jesus rebuked them sharply. He told them the greatest position was that of a servant. What a contrast to the kingdoms they were familiar with, in which strong individuals with political clout were considered the greatest.

How strange these words must have sounded to the disciples. Rome had been the controlling power in their lifetime. This imperial political kingdom was the only government they knew. They had heard of the past leadership of Israel's kings and judges, but Israel had not been an independent nation for a long time. They could not help but wonder if Jesus would restore independence to Israel. They could not imagine any other kind of kingdom.

In these discussions, Jesus did not deny that His Kingdom was coming. When the disciples asked pointedly if the Kingdom would be restored at this time, He introduced them to a more significant way of thinking: The *timing* of the Kingdom was not as important as the *power* of the Kingdom (Acts 1:7).

Jesus Proclaims the Power of His Kingdom

The day before Jesus' Ascension seemed liked the other days since the Resurrection. Conversation still centered on the Kingdom, but Jesus gave specific instructions about the power that would advance the Kingdom. The disciples were to return to Jerusalem and wait for the coming of the Holy Spirit, whom Jesus had talked about and the Father promised (Acts 1:4,5). This conversation only added to their questions about the Kingdom. In contrast to their desire for status based on personal abilities and talents, Jesus talked about the empowering presence of the Holy Spirit in the coming Kingdom.

What was the stated purpose of the coming of the Spirit?

The disciples would be used to build a Kingdom, but in a far different way than they imagined. When the Holy Spirit came, He would enable them to witness to the life, death, and resurrection of Jesus. The far-reaching effects of their witness would be believers in Christ throughout the entire world, in their generation and many generations to come.

In contrast to the kingdoms in that culture (and ours), the power of the kingdom of God would not come from strong personalities or talented individuals. Christ's Kingdom would advance by the endowment of the Holy Spirit's power upon individuals yielded to Him.

The Disciples Share the News of the Kingdom

After His final words to the disciples, Jesus was caught up into the clouds. Obediently, the disciples went back to Jerusalem and waited for the Spirit to fill them. After the Day of Pentecost, the disciples began sharing about Jesus. As Peter preached to the gathering crowd, he told them they were seeing the fulfillment of Kingdom promises going back as far as David's time (Acts 2:29–32).

The highlight of Peter's preaching that day was his open invitation: "Repent and be baptized . . . receive the gift of the Holy Spirit. The promise is for you and your children and for all who are far off—for all whom the Lord our God will call" (Acts 2:38,39).

The invitation to receive the Holy Spirit applied not only to those present on the Day of Pentecost, but also to anyone who is interested today. To a culture that encourages individualism, Jesus is still pointing to a better way to live. Instead of depending on self, depend on the Holy Spirit's power. It is the basic building block of the Kingdom, and will last forever.

On one of Jesus' last visits to the temple, He observed a widow putting two very small coins into the temple treasury and commended her for giving all she had. She stands as an example of a woman who worshipped with abandonment, demonstrating total dependency on God instead of self-sufficiency. Her act of worship is an encouragement to all who would learn dependency on the Holy Spirit rather than our selves, our talents, or our resources.

REFLECTING HIS IMAGE
Widow with Two Coins (Mark 12:41–44; Luke 21:1–4)

She made her way up the temple steps, staring at the coins in her hand, her last two coins. *Not much at all,* she thought.

Fingering her meager offering, she found a spot in the corner of the temple, out of the way. For a few minutes, she stood and watched. She watched the rich, the young, the "important people" pass by. Many dropped large amounts of money in the box.

What must their lives be like? she wondered in silence.

The last few years of her life were a burdensome blur because of the financial struggle she had suffered since her husband's death. With no family to support her, on some days she paused when she thought of the future. But not today. Today, her heart was full. Today, she wanted to give. Glancing down again at the only money she could call hers, she wondered if her pitiful offering would make a difference. And yet she knew God's eyes were on her. Her choice was to simply obey. Standing erect, she made her way past the crowd to the offering box.

The widow was not the only person people-watching in the temple. Close by, Jesus noticed the esteemed people in the court. His disciples saw only people, but His eyes saw life histories. He saw leaders and followers, husbands and wives, fathers and sons. Outwardly, many of them appeared successful and respectable, but His eyes could see through their disguises and He *knew* what their lives were like.

As the sound of the two copper coins resonated, Jesus looked up and saw the widow. He saw much more than a meager sacrifice. He saw abandoned dreams and withered hopes, and as He watched her fall to her knees and whisper a prayer to Jehovah Jireh, her Provider, Jesus seized the moment.

Earlier, with everyone listening, He had warned His disciples to watch out for religious scholars who took lavish pleasure in prominent positions and wanted to sit at the head of the table at church functions, all the while ignoring the weak and less fortunate. "The longer their prayers, the worse they get. But they'll pay for it in the end," Jesus said.[1]

Now, with His eyes fixed on the praying woman, Jesus continued to teach. "The plain truth is that this woman, this poor widow, has given by far the largest offering today. All these others gave offerings that 'they'll never miss; she gave extravagantly what she couldn't afford—she gave her all.'[2]"

A settled peace surrounded the woman in the midst of her quiet celebration, and as she stood to leave the temple, she felt safe, secure, and free! She brought everything she had and left with everything she needed. God was in control and He was her source.

And whether she realized it or not—the mighty Son of God *saw* and was moved by her total dependence on Him.

———————

[1]Mark 12:40, *The Message.*
[2]Mark 12:44, *The Message.*

EMBRACING THE PENTECOSTAL PERSPECTIVE
What is the Holy Spirit teaching me?

What does God see when He watches you? On more than one occasion, you have probably imitated the disciples at the Ascension—immobilized by loss, afraid of the future, paralyzed by a *"Now what?"* moment. But on your best days, He has caught you in the unsung moments of the widow's generosity. He sees when you change a diaper, wash the laundry, listen to a hurting friend, and give your time without expectation of something in return.

Now, wouldn't you like to live more of those "best" days? Imagine having a vision of something greater in front of you at all times, rather than the dreary landscape of a never-ending to do list. While angelic visitations—like the one the disciples received on that terrible-glorious day—are not the norm, catching God's vision can be. It begins with the realization that God has called each of us to fulfill a vital role in advancing His Kingdom.

Does the idea of God's personal, unique call on your life intimidate you? Why or why not?

What is the single most important need that must be met for you to fulfill God's call?

Left to our own devices, most of us return to the familiar or comfortable. And truth be told, we are often more interested in maintaining those conditions than we are in changing our lives or attempting something new. "Focusing on the self is the opposite of focusing on God. Anyone completely absorbed in self ignores God, ends up thinking more about self than God. That person ignores who God is and what he is doing."[1]

Do you struggle to put God's ways above your own? How so?

When are you most likely to give in to your own will?

Name one exciting change you have experienced. Is anything from this situation transferable to circumstances that you find more intimidating?

Just as the Lord reminded the disciples of His mission and their place in it, He also insisted that they first receive the baptism in the Holy Spirit. He specifically related this gift to a result (power) and a purpose (witness). Heroic acts of obedience—like those we see in the lives of the widow and disciples—do not occur intentionally without the fullness of the Spirit.

Are you availing yourself of the Spirit's power for your daily life?

---

[1] Romans 8:7, *The Message*.

Newer cars come with a warning bell that sounds when the gas tank nears empty. What signals your need for a fresh infilling of the Spirit?

INVITING GOD TO CHANGE MY VIEW
What change is God asking me to make?

Have you experienced the misfortune of an overzealous mailing list? It keeps the mailbox occupied, but adds little more than litter to your life. First come the full-price catalogs, where mild entertainment grows into temptation as items begin to appear irresistible. Then, the first sale catalog appears, offering a decent discount on one item, and the impulse to order builds to near action. Before a window of opportunity opens, yet another catalog arrives, with an even greater discount promised. Now approaching the "I'd be a fool not to" range of nearly 50 percent off, you schedule the order for the coming weekend—just in time for the clearance catalog to arrive. At this point, you decide, "Nah, I don't really think I need it!"

What is it about the psyche of discounting? Why is a clearance rack sometimes unappealing? While diehard shoppers do not allow the disarray of overlooked, damaged merchandise to discourage them, others pass by with little more than faint interest. The same applies to the act of discounting oneself. If you are empowered by discounting others, you will never know real power. If you discount yourself, you will never follow through on the conviction to act, thereby failing to experience true empowerment.

And while buyer's remorse may plague the novice or the careless shopper, such regret is completely foreign to the obedient, Spirit-led follower of Jesus Christ.

Do you need to be freed of the habit of discounting yourself or others? Would you like to know the empowerment of Spirit baptism? Have you intentionally placed yourself in a position to require God's strength above your own? Will you let go of your fear to embrace the Lord's power?

Prayer

Thank You for the wake-up call, Lord! I know You're watching me, just like You watched the widow at the temple that day. I want You to find me active, not immobilized by uncertainty or circumstance like the disciples just after Your Ascension. I want You to see gratitude, obedience, generosity, and power in my life. I don't come by those traits naturally, though, so I need the fullness of Your Spirit in my life. Fill me, Lord!

JOURNALING
Take a few minutes to record your personal insights from the lesson.

Her Answer to Pluralism

CATCHING SIGHT

Introduction

YOU MAY HAVE a friend who does not believe in Jesus, but she loves God, does many good deeds, and is very spiritual. She loves God. You love God. How can we say others are wrong and we're right? Are there any absolutes?

A music teacher can give us an example of an absolute. By tapping a certain tuning fork she can sound middle C. It was middle C yesterday; it will be middle C tomorrow; it will be middle C a thousand years from now—an absolute.

Tolerance used to mean that everyone has a right to their beliefs. But the new pluralism takes the idea of tolerance further and forbids anyone claiming that anyone else's belief is untrue. If we say someone is wrong we are considered intolerant and closed-minded.

We pray to God, the Three in One—who we know is God the Father, God the Son, and God the Holy Spirit. Because your friend doesn't recognize this truth doesn't make it untrue. If she doesn't believe in the Trinity, she does not recognize that Jesus is the "fullness of the Deity liv[ing] in bodily form" (Colossians 2:9).

There *are* absolutes. One absolute in the Christian faith is the complete divinity and complete humanity of Jesus Christ. Another is that the Scriptures, both Old and New Testaments, are verbally inspired of God and are the revelation of God to man, the infallible, authoritative rule of faith and conduct. If you do not believe in the Bible then there is no absolute on which you can base all other beliefs.

GETTING FOCUSED
Begin your study by considering the following:

If we agree that Jesus Christ and the Word of God are absolutes, what other absolutes can Christians agree on?

BIBLE READING
Acts 3:1–8,12–16; 4:8–12,18–20

New International Version

3:1 One day Peter and John were going up to the temple at the time of prayer—at three in the afternoon. 2 Now a man crippled from birth was being carried to the temple gate called Beautiful, where he was put every day to beg from those going into the temple courts. 3 When he saw Peter and John about to enter, he asked them for money. 4 Peter looked straight at him, as did John. Then Peter said, "Look at us!" 5 So the man gave them his attention, expecting to get something from them.

6 Then Peter said, "Silver or gold I do not have, but what I have I give you. In the name of Jesus Christ of Nazareth, walk." 7 Taking him by the right hand, he helped him up, and instantly the man's feet and ankles became strong. 8 He jumped to his feet and began to walk. Then he went with them into the temple courts, walking and jumping, and praising God.

12 When Peter saw this, he said to

New Living Translation

3:1 Peter and John went to the Temple one afternoon to take part in the three o'clock prayer service. 2 As they approached the Temple, a man lame from birth was being carried in. Each day he was put beside the Temple gate, the one called the Beautiful Gate, so he could beg from the people going into the Temple. 3 When he saw Peter and John about to enter, he asked them for some money.

4 Peter and John looked at him intently, and Peter said, "Look at us!" 5 The lame man looked at them eagerly, expecting a gift. 6 But Peter said, "I don't have any money for you. But I'll give you what I have. In the name of Jesus Christ of Nazareth, get up and walk!"

7 Then Peter took the lame man by the right hand and helped him up. And as he did, the man's feet and anklebones were healed and strengthened. 8 He jumped up, stood on his feet, and began to walk! Then, walking, leaping, and praising God,

New International Version

them: "Men of Israel, why does this surprise you? Why do you stare at us as if by our own power or godliness we had made this man walk? 13 The God of Abraham, Isaac and Jacob, the God of our fathers, has glorified his servant Jesus. You handed him over to be killed, and you disowned him before Pilate, though he had decided to let him go. 14 You disowned the Holy and Righteous One and asked that a murderer be released to you. 15 You killed the author of life, but God raised him from the dead. We are witnesses of this. 16 By faith in the name of Jesus, this man whom you see and know was made strong. It is Jesus' name and the faith that comes through him that has given this complete healing to him, as you can all see."

4:8 Then Peter, filled with the Holy Spirit, said to them: "Rulers and elders of the people! 9 If we are being called to account today for an act of kindness shown to a cripple and are asked how he was healed, 10 then know this, you and all the people of Israel: It is by the name of Jesus Christ of Nazareth, whom you crucified but whom God raised from the dead, that this man stands before you healed. 11 He is "'the stone you builders rejected, which has become the capstone.' 12 Salvation is found in no one else, for there is no other name under heaven given to men by which we must be saved."

New Living Translation

he went into the Temple with them.

12 Peter saw his opportunity and addressed the crowd. "People of Israel," he said, "what is so astounding about this? And why look at us as though we had made this man walk by our own power and godliness? 13 For it is the God of Abraham, the God of Isaac, the God of Jacob, the God of all our ancestors who has brought glory to his servant Jesus by doing this. This is the same Jesus whom you handed over and rejected before Pilate, despite Pilate's decision to release him. 14 You rejected this holy, righteous one and instead demanded the release of a murderer. 15 You killed the author of life, but God raised him to life. And we are witnesses of this fact!"

16 "The name of Jesus has healed this man—and you know how lame he was before. Faith in Jesus' name has caused this healing before your very eyes."

4:8 Then Peter, filled with the Holy Spirit, said to them, "Leaders and elders of our nation, 9 are we being questioned because we've done a good deed for a crippled man? Do you want to know how he was healed? 10 Let me clearly state to you and to all the people of Israel that he was healed in the name and power of Jesus Christ from Nazareth, the man you crucified, but whom God raised from the dead. 11 For Jesus is the one referred to in the Scriptures,

New International Version

18 Then they called them in again and commanded them not to speak or teach at all in the name of Jesus. 19 But Peter and John replied, "Judge for yourselves whether it is right in God's sight to obey you rather than God. 20 For we cannot help speaking about what we have seen and heard."

New Living Translation

where it says, 'The stone that you builders rejected has now become the cornerstone.' 12 There is salvation in no one else! There is no other name in all of heaven for people to call on to save them."

18 So they called the apostles back in and told them never again to speak or teach about Jesus.

19 But Peter and John replied, "Do you think God wants us to obey you rather than him? 20 We cannot stop telling about the wonderful things we have seen and heard."

GAINING BIBLICAL INSIGHT

Dispelling spiritual confusion

A world filled with religious diversity challenges the absolute claim of Christianity that Jesus is the only divine Son of God. The Christian's response is that Jesus is who He claimed to be and He demonstrates His divinity by confirming His Word.

A study of the Early Church reveals that those who walked with Jesus were thoroughly convinced of His deity. They exalted His name by expressing their faith boldly and suffering persecution willingly. He honored their faith by using them to perform miracles through the power of the Holy Spirit.

The Power of Jesus' Name

In the days following the Day of Pentecost, believers spent much time together in prayer and studying the Scriptures. The first miracle recorded in the Book of Acts happened as Peter and John went to the temple for a regular time of prayer. They were confronted by a man who was regularly brought to the temple gate to beg as a means of livelihood. While the disciples could not respond to his request for money, they perceived his greater need for wholeness.

Peter's first response to the man's request for money was: "Look at us!" His intent is unclear. His reply, "Silver or gold I do not have," could imply he was thinking, *Do we look like we have any money?* Or he may have been commanding the man's attention for what he wanted to tell him. Peter quickly followed his declaration with, "but what I have I give you. In the name of Jesus Christ of Nazareth, walk."

In the days before Christ's crucifixion, the disciples spent many hours listening to Him teach. After His death, resurrection, and ascension, they spent time remembering His teachings and searching Scriptures. Peter possibly remembered Jesus saying: "Anyone who has faith in me will do what I have been doing" (John 14:12) and other similar teachings. Peter had seen Jesus as He "went around doing good and healing all who were under the power of the devil, because God was with him" (Acts 10:38). The instant Peter perceived the man's need, he realized he *did* have something to give to the man—the wholeness only Jesus brings. He acted on the authority of Jesus' name and the miracle happened.

The Power of Witnessing in His Name

Public response to the miracle was instantaneous. Crowds immediately bombarded Peter and John with questions and adulation. Peter dealt with any temptation to self-exaltation by taking the opportunity to witness about the power of Jesus' name. Boldly, he confronted the people with their sin of rejecting Jesus, declaring this miracle resulted from faith in His name.

Reading Peter's message to the crowd that day gives us insight into effective witnessing to people of other beliefs. This crowd would have been primarily Jews who came to worship in the temple. Peter built his witness on their knowledge of God from their history, and pointed them to Jesus (Acts 3:13). Note how clearly, yet graciously, he declared the message to the people. He attributed their error of rejecting Jesus to lack of knowledge (verse 17) and showed them how to amend their ways through repentance (verse 19). In this message, Peter demonstrated how to declare truth boldly and maintain a right spirit.

The Conflict of Witnessing for His Name

When we do things in what we consider the right way, we assume we will have a positive response. However, Peter and John found this was not necessarily so.

What were the various reactions to Peter's message?

This momentous day was not only the occasion of the first apostolic miracle; it was also the day of the first recorded suffering for the message of Jesus. While many people believed the message, the Jewish leadership was greatly disturbed. As a result of witnessing for the power of Jesus' name, Peter and John were put in jail for the night and vigorously questioned the next day.

How did the apostles respond to this unexpected turn of events?

Unfair treatment often reveals the character of the ones being mistreated. Rather than responding angrily or with self-pity, Peter responded boldly in the power of the Spirit, reaffirming the importance of Jesus' name. "Salvation is found in no one else, for there is no other name under heaven given to men by which we must be saved" (Acts 4:12).

Peter's statement clearly delineates the Christian position that Jesus stands alone as the Son of God and trusting Him is the *only* means of salvation. The apostles were so convinced of this truth that they were willing to suffer for His name. When the religious leaders told them they could not speak or teach in the name of Jesus, they replied courteously but firmly that they must obey God. From history, we know most of the apostles were martyred because of their commitment.

The Determination to Exalt His Name

Following the events of these two days, Peter and John returned to the place where other believers were gathered. They had a victorious report and an ominous one. The growth of the Church might have stopped there had the disciples submitted to the threats of those who arrested them. Instead, they joined in prayer with other believers, exalting the name of Jesus. Consequently, they received a fresh infilling of the Holy Spirit, which gave them boldness to continue declaring the Word of God.

Maintaining our faith through times of opposition and discouragement may be a challenge. Matthew gives an example of a woman who persevered in faith in spite of resistance. Jesus commended her as a woman of great faith.

REFLECTING HIS IMAGE
Canaanite Woman (Matthew 15:21–28)

What was I thinking? I pushed myself toward Him. Did I think I deserved special consideration? Is it any wonder Jesus' disciples became agitated with me?

I had legitimate questions, and as a mother, I would do almost anything for the love of my daughter. My child was suffering. It didn't matter that I am a Canaanite and He is a Jew. She was being tormented by a demon, I was desperate, and I could not have cared less about society's rules. I knew positively Jesus could put an end to our agony!

My daughter's erratic behavior began some time ago. At first, the signs were subtle, but over time, the fits of rage and self-inflicted wounds were so severe she required around-the-clock care. My beautiful, loving girl became a shell living in a tormented haze, and every year seemed worse than the last. I remember the days I watched helplessly as she sat on the floor in the corner of the room, rocking back and forth, back and forth, moaning and cursing continuously.

But the nightmares were the worst. Her superhuman strength made it impossible for me to handle her, so eventually I had to tie her down just to control her. Can you imagine? Imprisoning your own child. The anguish of these episodes was almost more than I could bear. Almost.

I knew Jesus was in town that day, although I learned later He came from Galilee to be *alone* with His disciples. I considered all the reasons why I might be turned away if I tried to seek His help. I knew that, as a Jew, He had strict rules controlling His contact with people from other nations. After all, my people had been enemies of the Jews for hundreds of years and He might decide to avoid me altogether, since I was a pagan and had no personal relationship with God.

But somehow, none of that mattered. I had heard of this man, Jesus, and the miracles He performed, and all I could visualize was my daughter—well, fully clothed, and in her right mind. No one would stop me from finding Jesus. No one!

I guess it was desperation that pushed me forward when I first approached Him that morning. Wanting to draw His attention, I pleaded to Him as "Lord, Son of David." I shouted as loud as I could, over and over again, for Jesus to have mercy on me. I cried to Him that my daughter was suffering terribly from demon possession.

A quiet hush followed. Jesus looked right through me, but didn't answer. That's when His disciples stepped in and asked Him to "take care of me" so I would go away and stop bothering them.

Afraid He might refuse me, I came closer to Him and this time I knelt at His feet and—for the first time in my life—I begged! I addressed Him simply as "Lord" and I *begged* Him to heal my daughter.

Jesus' response was unexpected. He told me it wasn't right to take children's bread and throw it to the dogs. My answer came from somewhere deep within me as I replied, "That may be true, but even dogs eat the crumbs that fall from their master's table."

It must have been the cry in my voice and the desperate look on my face, because in that moment He knew this Gentile woman was not going to give up, or back down, or walk away!

As confusing as the social conventions of the day were, I didn't care what Jesus or His disciples thought of my loud, obnoxious mannerisms. I only knew my sweet daughter needed help and Jesus could help her. It was that simple!

Later that day, I washed and brushed my daughter's hair and changed her clothes. Holding her quietly in my arms for the first time in years, I looked into eyes that were clear. I touched hands that were not shaking. Jesus had met me at my greatest point of need. He healed my child. And I smiled as I heard words coming from my daughter that every mother of a sick child longs to hear: "Mama, I'm hungry. May I please have something to eat?"

EMBRACING THE PENTECOSTAL PERSPECTIVE
What is the Holy Spirit teaching me?

Hunger is a powerful motivator. It drove a lame man to ignore humiliation and beg day after day at the Beautiful Gate, and it propelled a desperate mother through a multitude of lesser options to the only One who could meet her need. Today, we are surrounded by hungry people—specifically, people who are hungry for spiritual fulfillment. In this climate, Pentecostals have unprecedented opportunities to deliver the Bread of Life.

At the same time, we face a world of religious diversity.

•*Pluralism*: All ways lead to God and none is superior to the others.

•*Postmodernism*: One characteristic is questioning the existence of truth.

•*Tolerance*: No longer just respectful of religious freedom, this concept insists that no religion can identify another as wrong or claim to be the only true way.

All of these contribute to spiritual confusion in the midst of spiritual hunger.

If acting only on an emotional level, the Gentile mother would have quit a thousand times. Facing an unfamiliar crowd, pushing forward, making a spectacle of herself, seeing the unwelcome stares of the disciples, and even hearing Jesus' initial response had to bring discouragement. Yet she persisted! Would you?

You may feel unwelcome when witnessing. Nobody wants to be disliked, but are you more afraid of what people think of you than what God thinks of you? What do you do with your fear?

The Canaanite mother acted out of love and desperation. Do you love the lost? Are you desperate to see others saved? What do you do to show this love?

"What I have I give you." Peter's words to the crippled man challenge us today. Postmoderns look for the supernatural and crave the mystery of faith. They are ripe for a move of God's Spirit. We should avoid offering dogmatism, defensiveness, or haughty attitudes. These are the tools of fearful people, not Spirit-filled people. Peter had no fear when he invited this man to experience God's life-giving power—*Peter had the Spirit of God!*

Could you say what Peter did? What do you have to give?

How can you give God more room in your life to operate in His power?

George Buttrick, former Harvard chaplain, sometimes faced antagonistic students in his office. They would challenge him with blunt declarations: "I don't believe in God." Buttrick would calmly invite the latest would-be atheist to have a seat and tell him about the God he or she did not believe in, adding that he probably didn't believe in that God either. Buttrick was then able to share the reality and power of the living God! He understood how to witness with confidence and kindness, not compromise.

Biblical illiteracy statistics have hit record highs with corresponding percentages of people questioning biblical authority. Simply quoting John 14:6 or Acts 4:12 will not convince a pluralist that Jesus saves. So how will you present the gospel?

Christians have been accused of being "all mouth and no ears." Why is listening important in sharing the gospel?

INVITING GOD TO CHANGE MY VIEW
What change is God asking me to make?

Following the helpful directions of the attendants, two friends parked alongside thousands of others in the vast hay field. Anticipating a day of fun and relaxation followed by a phenomenal display of fireworks, neither gave a thought to noting the position of their car. Hours later, facing the impromptu parking lot now completely filled and lit by nothing more than moonlight and headlights, a feeling of dismay threatened. How in the world could they have forgotten to look for landmarks? Other than chance or divine direction, how would they locate their car?

Amazingly, within just moments, they were climbing into their vehicle. Prayer, coupled with strategic questioning, had led them to the car. They knew what time they had arrived, so by asking others when they had parked, the friends were able to narrow the search area drastically. Accurate navigation always requires two points of reference. For believers navigating the present spiritual confusion, those two points are Jesus and the mission of God.

Knowing Jesus personally and understanding who He is—the Son of God, unique in His incarnation, sinless life, selfless death, resurrection, and impartation of the Spirit—enables us to stand firmly. One cannot embrace all faiths as equally valid without stripping Jesus of His unique identity. Second, understanding that God's mission requires us to share the Good News with others means never questioning our right to witness. People without Christ will perish. We as Christians cannot succumb to the demands of political correctness or explicit scorn.

Do you know Jesus Christ as your Lord and Savior? Can you explain why Jesus is unique from the gods of other religions? Do you realize you have a role to fulfill in God's mission? Are you obediently serving in God's mission? Do you need more of the Spirit's power and love to make you an effective witness? Will you ask the Spirit to identify any arrogance or other personal hindrance to your outreach efforts?

Prayer

Father, I want to be a powerful witness for You in these exciting days of opportunity. I want to know Jesus more and more. Help me view others with compassion, rather than as potential conquests. Give me discernment to hear and understand what people are saying, so I can help them embrace the Truth. Forgive me for retreating to the non-threatening witness of lifestyle alone. Let my words be true, my life full of integrity, and my witness effective. Amen.

JOURNALING
Take a few minutes to record your personal insights from the lesson.

Her Response to Materialism

CATCHING SIGHT
Introduction

Many years ago when the United States was young, word reached the eastern states that people living in the West had found gold, and lots of it. Thousands of people sold their homes, loaded their possessions in wagons, and headed west. They faced many dangers—many died on the way and only a few really found gold.

One man found a lot of gold and decided to go back east to spend it. As he and others were crossing the Mississippi River, the boat struck a rock and sank. It was close enough to shore for most people to swim to safety, but many drowned including the newly rich miner. He was known to be a good swimmer and the survivors wondered why he drowned.

When his body was recovered, they discovered that he was wearing a belt with many pockets, all crammed with gold nuggets. The extra weight caused his death. He had enough time to take off the belt, but he didn't want to give up that gold so he allowed it to drag him to a watery grave.

Materialism can both entice and enslave us if our motives are not in line with God's desires.

A terrible tragedy occurred when the miner lost his life because he was unwilling to give up his gold. It is no less a tragedy when someone becomes so interested in the things of the world that she no longer has time to look after her spiritual safety.

GETTING FOCUSED

Begin your study by considering the following:

Can you honestly say that God, not money, is your master? One test is to ask which one occupies more of your thoughts, time, and efforts.

BIBLE READING

Acts 4:32–37; 5:1–11

New International Version

4:32 All the believers were one in heart and mind. No one claimed that any of his possessions was his own, but they shared everything they had. 33 With great power the apostles continued to testify to the resurrection of the Lord Jesus, and much grace was upon them all. 34 There were no needy persons among them. For from time to time those who owned lands or houses sold them, brought the money from the sales 35 and put it at the apostles' feet, and it was distributed to anyone as he had need.

36 Joseph, a Levite from Cyprus, whom the apostles called Barnabas (which means Son of Encouragement), 37 sold a field he owned and brought the money and put it at the apostles' feet.

5:1 Now a man named Ananias, together with his wife Sapphira, also sold a piece of property. 2 With his wife's full knowledge he kept back part of the money for himself, but brought the rest and put it at the apostles' feet.

New Living Translation

4:32 All the believers were of one heart and mind, and they felt that what they owned was not their own; they shared everything they had. 33 And the apostles gave powerful witness to the resurrection of the Lord Jesus, and God's great favor was upon them all. 34 There was no poverty among them, because people who owned land or houses sold them 35 and brought the money to the apostles to give to others in need.

36 For instance, there was Joseph, the one the apostles nicknamed Barnabas (which means "Son of Encouragement"). He was from the tribe of Levi and came from the island of Cyprus. 37 He sold a field he owned and brought the money to the apostles for those in need.

5:1 There was also a man named Ananias who, with his wife, Sapphira, sold some property. 2 He brought part of the money to the apostles, but he claimed it was the full amount. His wife had agreed to this deception.

New International Version

3 Then Peter said, "Ananias, how is it that Satan has so filled your heart that you have lied to the Holy Spirit and have kept for yourself some of the money you received for the land? 4 Didn't it belong to you before it was sold? And after it was sold, wasn't the money at your disposal? What made you think of doing such a thing? You have not lied to men but to God."

5 When Ananias heard this, he fell down and died. And great fear seized all who heard what had happened. 6 Then the young men came forward, wrapped up his body, and carried him out and buried him.

7 About three hours later his wife came in, not knowing what had happened. 8 Peter asked her, "Tell me, is this the price you and Ananias got for the land?"

"Yes," she said, "that is the price."

9 Peter said to her, "How could you agree to test the Spirit of the Lord? Look! The feet of the men who buried your husband are at the door, and they will carry you out also."

10 At that moment she fell down at his feet and died. Then the young men came in and, finding her dead, carried her out and buried her beside her husband. 11 Great fear seized the whole church and all who heard about these events.

New Living Translation

3 Then Peter said, "Ananias, why has Satan filled your heart? You lied to the Holy Spirit, and you kept some of the money for yourself. 4 The property was yours to sell or not sell, as you wished. And after selling it, the money was yours to give away. How could you do a thing like this? You weren't lying to us but to God."

5 As soon as Ananias heard these words, he fell to the floor and died. Everyone who heard about it was terrified. 6 Then some young men wrapped him in a sheet and took him out and buried him.

7 About three hours later his wife came in, not knowing what had happened. 8 Peter asked her, "Was this the price you and your husband received for your land?"

"Yes," she replied, "that was the price."

9 And Peter said, "How could the two of you even think of doing a thing like this—conspiring together to test the Spirit of the Lord? Just outside that door are the young men who buried your husband, and they will carry you out, too."

10 Instantly, she fell to the floor and died. When the young men came in and saw that she was dead, they carried her out and buried her beside her husband. 11 Great fear gripped the entire church and all others who heard what had happened.

GAINING BIBLICAL INSIGHT
Living in contentment

Many people would disagree with the belief that the physical world of material things is the only reality. They would assert their conviction that the spiritual world also exists. However, in practice many of these same people could be defined as materialists because of their preoccupation with material things, rather than intellectual or spiritual realities. Too often, time and energy are spent in relentless pursuit of the accumulation of material comforts while spiritual and intellectual concerns are ignored. A study of the Early Church's dealings with materialism can help us develop a biblical response to the demands of materialism in our culture.

Prevailing Attitudes in the Early Church

After the miracle of healing at the Beautiful Gate, believers met together regularly for prayer and worship. Having experienced the Spirit's empowerment on the Day of Pentecost, the believers were eager to hear the apostles' teaching of the Word of God to understand more about Him. According to the Scripture, "the apostles performed many miraculous signs and wonders" during these sessions together (Acts 5:12).

God's blessing produced a unity of spirit as the believers met. Their focus was not on themselves, but on God. Their personal lives were consumed with the overarching work God was doing among them. Their generosity with material goods was the practical result of their vibrant spiritual condition.

While the believers were generous with the needy, they still maintained their own homes where they met together. Generosity and hospitality characterized their relationships with one another, but this does not imply communal living with no private ownership of property. Surplus possessions were sold to provide for the needy, but the believers maintained their own private residences.

Barnabas is mentioned as an individual who used his material possessions for the public good. His generous act of selling a field and bringing the money to the apostles probably was repeated by many others who had this capability. His good example serves as a stark contrast to the actions of Ananias and Sapphira.

Problems Arise among the Believers

In the midst of this great spiritual blessing, the carnal nature of one couple was revealed. In what appears to be an attempt to imitate the gracious action of Barnabas, Ananias and Sapphira also sold some property, but they kept some of the money.

Why was Ananias's action wrong?

Keeping the money was not wrong according to Peter's questions. The hypocritical act of pretending to bring the total proceeds of the sale to the apostles was wrong.

Note how one sinful act led to another. Ananias's deceitful actions were followed with lying words. Peter's denouncement of these sins reminded Ananias (and all of us) that his sin was not against man but against God.

Judgment fell on Ananias because of his deceitful act, the first recorded sin of the Church Age. This swift judgment can be compared to the sudden judgment of Nadab and Abihu, Aaron's sons, at the beginning of the Aaronic priesthood (Leviticus 10:1,2). The message in both cases is sin brings judgment.

The inclusion of the sequel to Ananias's actions, by his wife Sapphira, emphasizes individual accountability. Sapphira was given opportunity to tell the truth to the apostles, but she followed her husband's example of deceitfulness and hypocrisy and suffered the consequences of her own sinfulness.

What possible motives could Ananias and Sapphira have had for their actions?

Dealing with Covetousness, the Root of the Problem

Though other motives may have been driving them also, it is obvious that Ananias and Sapphira loved money more than they loved truth. They put more value on their possessions than on their relationships with the apostles or with God.

In his letter to Timothy, Paul warns that all kinds of evil can come from covetousness, the inordinate desire for things. "For the love of money is a root of all kinds of evil. Some people, eager for money, have wandered from the faith and pierced themselves with many griefs" (1 Timothy 6:10).

According to this Scripture, where is the problem?

The problem is not with money itself or other material possessions. The problem is the attitude—an excessive affection for money or the things it can buy.

Early in His ministry, Jesus instructed the disciples about the proper attitude toward material things. In the Sermon on the Mount, He taught them not to worry about the basic provisions of life, because God was their provider (Matthew 6:25–34). Throughout His ministry,

He emphasized principles of good stewardship with many parables. He warned against greed, teaching that life was not measured by material possessions: "Be on your guard against all kinds of greed; a man's life does not consist in the abundance of his possessions" (Luke 12:15). He wanted them to live in contentment, confident that God would supply their needs.

Paul followed Jesus' example, encouraging Christians to develop the practice of generosity. He taught that the purpose of working was not to have money to spend on ourselves, but to have something to give to others. "He who has been stealing must steal no longer, but must work, doing something useful with his own hands, that he may have something to share with those in need" (Ephesians 4:28).

While others may work that they might *have*, Christians use what they gain to *give*. They own their possessions, but their possessions do not own them.

One of the sad stories in Scripture tells of Lot's wife, a woman whose love of things brought tragic results. Her materialistic attitude and apparent disbelief of God's Word through His messenger caused her to lose her life.

REFLECTING HIS IMAGE
Lot's Wife (Genesis 19:1–26)

Lot's wife stared off into the distance, stoic as stone and white as salt. She had been prominent and prosperous—but she didn't finish well.

Mrs. Lot scanned the crowd at the marketplace. Dozens of people pushed past her, many of them nodding, many of them moving one way or another to make a path. As she made her way, a plastic smile crossed her face. *Sodom is my home,* she thought. *These are my friends. My children were born here. This is all I know.*

As she relived the past few hours, she couldn't help but look back on her life and consider all she stood to lose. A confusing mix of helplessness, anger, and sorrow coursed through her as she shook her head in disbelief. The love and attachment Lot's wife felt for her home and possessions caused an ache in the pit of her stomach. *Leave here? Abandon everything? How can my husband ask such a thing?* she wondered.

As a young married couple, the Lots could not have had a better beginning. Such hope the two of them had. Such amazing dreams they dreamed together. Mrs. Lot had a godly husband; she had Abraham and Sarah as an uncle and aunt by marriage and—aside from their wealth—she had their faith, knowledge, and prayers, which were no small privileges.

Even so, eventually relocating to Sodom in the affluent Jordan plain was not a hard thing for her to do. Together, the Lots put down roots. Her husband was industrious and hardworking; it's what he knew and loved to do. And Mrs. Lot reaped the benefits—a beautiful household and recognition as the wife of a city leader.

In the beginning, the Lots were able to ignore the heaviness in the air that seemed to pervade everything and everyone who lived in Sodom. A darkness surrounded the city and a stench surrounded its people, while Mr. and Mrs. Lot tried not to notice the sin of it all.

Over time, however, Sodom's culture became *their* culture. Pangs of conscience reminded them of Uncle Abraham's good example and how he had taught his family not to set their hearts on material things. But the woman who, many years before, had come to Sodom's marketplace as a stranger, now prided herself as one of its chief citizens.

"What should I pack? Where are we going? What about my things, my friends, the rest of my life?" Lot's wife mumbled to her servants as she hurried along.

Arriving back home, she bustled around the house, going in circles, accomplishing little, and wishing she had a few minutes to herself. *Not a good time for overnight company,* she thought as she eyed the two visitors who shared a meal at *her* table.

Later that night she clutched a prized box of spices to her chest. Slowly, carefully, she placed it on the floor. She pressed her fingers to her tired eyes, trying to push away the confusion that plagued her. *Too much to think about.* She was tired. She needed to rest.

Loud voices shook her from a fretful sleep just after dawn.

"Wake up. Hurry. Take your wife and daughters and lead them safely out of the city or they will die," the two guests shouted to her husband. "God is going to destroy Sodom for its wickedness. Leave now! And whatever you do, don't look back!"

A chill enveloped Lot's wife as she staggered to her feet, half-dazed. What happened next was a confused blur as a hand grabbed her arm and pulled her forward to the outside gate. "Hurry, hurry! Faster, faster! Go now!" the voice shouted.

Her legs felt weak as willows as she lunged forward, trying to gain her footing. Moments later, she found herself in the shadowed street being dragged out of the city.

An eerie darkness filled the sky. *Did the men say* destroy *Sodom?* she wondered. *Surely they did not mean* destroy. Again, she heard voices coming from behind her.

"Run for your life! Don't look back! Don't stop anywhere on the plain—run for the hills or you'll be swept away."[1]

By now she was hysterical. "Lot! Lot!" she cried. She called and called, but there was no response. If anything, the silence seemed to deepen. *Hurry, faster, faster,* she told herself.

Her heart beat wildly as she ran. Suddenly, a thunderous bolt shook the earth and then a river of lava from God began to fall from the sky.

All at once, her thoughts turned to her house, her things, her friends, the young men who were engaged to her daughters—the rest of her life! *My heart is still in Sodom,* she whispered to herself.

Panting and out of breath, she stopped abruptly as a strange calm gripped her. She turned, and looked back to her city—back to Sodom.

As she wept salty tears, her eyes became fixed. Her countenance changed and she died there, stoic as stone and white as salt.

---

[1]Genesis 19:17, *The Message.*

EMBRACING THE PENTECOSTAL PERSPECTIVE
What is the Holy Spirit teaching me?

A wife stood penitently before her husband as he reviewed the receipt from her purchase at an expensive leather purse outlet. "We're going to have to take out a second mortgage!" he groused. She hung her head in despair. "I know. I really shouldn't have bought three."

The old adage, "You can't have too much of a good thing," actually applies to very few things, and all of them are nonmaterial. Whether your weakness is clothing, accessories, or food, excess can cause profound physical, financial, relationship, and emotional problems, all of which weaken spiritual health.

Materialism confirms a crisis of focus. Sapphira looked straight ahead and lied in an effort to hoard money. Lot's wife looked back and paid the ultimate price. Colossians 3:2 says, "Set your minds on things above, not on earthly things." Only the Spirit can bring the transformation that makes this focus possible.

Are you satisfied with your current standard of living? Could you make do with less? Explain your answers.

How can a materially-guided focus destroy right priorities and weaken your family or ministry?

Are you willing to postpone a major purchase in order to advance the Kingdom through your giving?

Another way to respond to materialistic tendencies is to remind yourself of who you are in Christ. Some distort this identity and actually feed materialism, using scriptural promises as blank checks for prosperity. Such misinterpretation not only violates the integrity of God's Word, but also robs the believer of the profound wealth to be had in finding one's identity and security in relationship to the Savior. It creates an improper vulnerability, making one susceptible to finding prestige in position or possession.

Describe the "riches in Christ Jesus" from the great promise of Philippians 4:19.

What does "keeping up with the Joneses" look like in your world?

How can we hold one another accountable for materialistic thinking?

Some time ago, a series of commercials showed various awkward conversations in which one person insulted the other. To get out of the situation, that person simply responded, "Thank you." It made no sense in the context of the conversation, but it completely changed the offended person's attitude. While you may not repair a rift so easily, the principle of gratitude truly has the power to effect change. You can maintain a heart of gratitude, being thankful for what you do have, not coveting what you do not have.

How do you model gratitude for everyday comforts (your home, meals, wardrobe, etc.)?

Is thanking God in less-than-ideal circumstances helpful or hypocritical? Why?

How can you gently redirect another person's negative focus?

INVITING GOD TO CHANGE MY VIEW
What change is God asking me to make?

Fearing the strict weight limitations, the traveler tried to look nonchalant as she struggled to hoist her suitcase on the scale at the counter. Before she could rejoice over meeting the restriction, the airline representative remarked dryly, "They don't have concrete blocks where you're going? You have to take your own?" Her traveling companion nearly fell over laughing!

Women—not all, but many—have a special talent for overpacking. Most of us have unpacked a suitcase in which nearly half of the items went untouched. Why? It could be the remnant of a childhood spent in Girl Scouts, adhering to the "Be Prepared" motto. It might be the tendency to prepare for every type of activity and weather possible on a trip. But it *might* be an indicator of materialism.

When having the perfect outfit or pair of shoes for every occasion takes precedent over preparing our hearts and minds, we have a problem. If your interest in "things" outweighs your hunger for a close relationship with God, you need to ask Him to help you deal with materialism.

Ask the Holy Spirit to search your heart. Do you need to hold the stuff of this world a little more loosely? Would you like to demonstrate with your time and money that your priorities are aligned with God's Word? Are you giving as generously as you can?

Prayer

Father, thank You for dealing with real things. As difficult as it is to admit, I sometimes get too wrapped up in the stuff of this life. I would hate for heaven to be less occupied because I was too occupied with shopping or something equally trivial. You warned us that we could not serve two masters, and today I want to reaffirm that You are the One for me! Let Kingdom life and Kingdom priorities hold my focus steadfast. Amen.

JOURNALING

Take a few minutes to record your personal insights from the lesson.

Her Approach to Diversity

CATCHING SIGHT

Introduction

FOUR MEN STOOD together admiring Niagara Falls. Although all four had the same view, each saw something different. One man was an artist and all he could see was the beauty of the scenery. Another man was a farmer and he thought of the ways his farm could use some of the water if it could be diverted into irrigation ditches. A third man was an engineer and, as he watched the strong currents, he calculated the wonderful electrical power the falls could generate. The fourth man was a minister and he thought of how wonderful the great Creator must be to create such a river and keep it running century after century.

As a rule, we see what we look for. Have you heard this little verse? "Two men looked through prison bars; one saw mud, the other stars."

At the close of a great sermon, a schoolteacher went up to the minister and said, "I counted eight grammatical errors in your sermon." The critic knew what was wrong with the sermon, but missed what was right with it—a message of love, faith, and salvation from sin.

As we go through life, we should make a habit of looking for the good, the true, and the beautiful in every situation and every person. We will see it if we look for it.

God can choose anyone—any age, nationality, or gender—to accomplish great things. Don't let your prejudices get in the way of people God has called.

GETTING FOCUSED

Begin your study by considering the following:

What are some avenues for embracing cultural diversity in your community?

BIBLE READING

Acts 6:1–6; 1 Corinthians 3:1–7

New International Version

Acts 6:1 In those days when the number of disciples was increasing, the Grecian Jews among them complained against the Hebraic Jews because their widows were being overlooked in the daily distribution of food. 2 So the Twelve gathered all the disciples together and said, "It would not be right for us to neglect the ministry of the word of God in order to wait on tables. 3 Brothers, choose seven men from among you who are known to be full of the Spirit and wisdom. We will turn this responsibility over to them 4 and will give our attention to prayer and the ministry of the word."

5 This proposal pleased the whole group. They chose Stephen, a man full of faith and of the Holy Spirit; also Philip, Procorus, Nicanor, Timon, Parmenas, and Nicolas from Antioch, a convert to Judaism. 6 They presented these men to the apostles, who prayed and laid their hands on them.

1 Corinthians 3:1 Brothers, I could not address you as spiritual but as worldly—mere infants in Christ.

New Living Translation

Acts 6:1 But as the believers rapidly multiplied, there were rumblings of discontent. Those who spoke Greek complained against those who spoke Hebrew, saying that their widows were being discriminated against in the daily distribution of food. 2 So the Twelve called a meeting of all the believers.

"We apostles should spend our time preaching and teaching the word of God, not administering a food program," they said. 3 "Now look around among yourselves, brothers, and select seven men who are well respected and are full of the Holy Spirit and wisdom. We will put them in charge of this business. 4 Then we can spend our time in prayer and preaching and teaching the word."

5 This idea pleased the whole group, and they chose the following: Stephen (a man full of faith and the Holy Spirit), Philip, Procorus, Nicanor, Timon, Parmenas, and Nicolas of Antioch (a Gentile convert to the Jewish faith, who had now become a Christian). 6 These seven

New International Version

2 I gave you milk, not solid food, for you were not yet ready for it. Indeed, you are still not ready. 3 You are still worldly. For since there is jealousy and quarreling among you, are you not worldly? Are you not acting like mere men? 4 For when one says, "I follow Paul," and another, "I follow Apollos," are you not mere men?

5 What, after all, is Apollos? And what is Paul? Only servants, through whom you came to believe—as the Lord has assigned to each his task. 6 I planted the seed, Apollos watered it, but God made it grow. 7 So neither he who plants nor he who waters is anything, but only God, who makes things grow.

New Living Translation

were presented to the apostles, who prayed for them as they laid their hands on them.

1 Corinthians 3:1 Dear brothers and sisters, when I was with you I couldn't talk to you as I would to mature Christians. I had to talk as though you belonged to this world or as though you were infants in the Christian life. 2 I had to feed you with milk and not with solid food, because you couldn't handle anything stronger. And you still aren't ready, 3 for you are still controlled by your own sinful desires. You are jealous of one another and quarrel with each other. Doesn't that prove you are controlled by your own desires? You are acting like people who don't belong to the Lord. 4 When one of you says, "I am a follower of Paul," and another says, "I prefer Apollos," aren't you acting like those who are not Christians?

5 Who is Apollos, and who is Paul, that we should be the cause of such quarrels? Why, we're only servants. Through us God caused you to believe. Each of us did the work the Lord gave us. 6 My job was to plant the seed in your hearts, and Apollos watered it, but it was God, not we, who made it grow. 7 The ones who do the planting or watering aren't important, but God is important because he is the one who makes the seed grow.

GAINING BIBLICAL INSIGHT
Embracing cultural differences

The central truth of Christianity is to love God with all our heart, soul, mind, and spirit, and our neighbor as ourselves. We hear this truth so often that it can become a platitude to which we give little thought. Loving others is easy as long as they look, act, and think like we do, and enjoy what we enjoy. But when someone is different, we may have problems loving her.

Modern technology has turned our world into a global village. Our next-door neighbors may not speak our language, dress like we do, eat what we eat, or value what we value. Yet they may love the Lord and come to our church. Even people from similar socioeconomic and cultural backgrounds may enjoy vastly different styles of worship. Today's believer is called to embrace cultural differences within the framework of the Church in Christian love. Prejudice has no place in the Christian community.

Cultural Differences in the Early Church

Cultural differences are not unique to our society. The young church in Jerusalem faced this dynamic shortly after Pentecost. A feeding program, established for widows among the believers, encountered difficulty because of language differences. Most of the Early Church converts were Jewish Christians with only a few Gentile proselytes. The Jews, however, did not all speak the same language. Some spoke Greek because they were descended from Jews in Greek-speaking nations, while those with Palestinian backgrounds spoke Aramaic.

With language differences came cultural differences. Although all these people were believers, they identified most closely with their own language group and its familiar customs. From these culturally different groups, we have the first report of discord within the Christian community. The Grecian Jews insisted their widows were being neglected in the daily distribution of food.

A similar division among Christians arose a few years later in Corinth. Here, the Christians separated into groups not because of cultural differences, but out of loyalty to the leaders who had introduced them to Christianity.

From what you know of the ministries of Apollos and Paul, what differences might have been found in these groups of Christians?

Apollos was what we might call a "silver-tongued orator." Paul, by his own admission, did not have an impressive personal appearance. His style of ministry was that of a teacher. Both preaching and teaching ministries are very important in the Church, but people sometimes are drawn to one type or the other. In Corinth, the people separated themselves according to their preferred style of leadership, which may have included different worship styles.

Confronting the Differences

Sometimes when problems arise among Christians, we overlook them out of a desire to preserve unity—an appropriate behavior in some instances. In both of these scriptural cases, however, major problems needed to be confronted. Different methods were used in each situation.

How was the discord problem handled in the Jerusalem church?

The apostles realized the church had grown beyond their ability to minister to all its needs. They decided to ask others to take leadership of the food distribution. Seven men were chosen to lead and ensure fairness in the daily distribution. These men are often referred to as the first deacons.

All the men chosen to serve had Greek names. Some people believe this implies they were all Grecian Jews. We cannot say this absolutely because some Hebrew-speaking Jews used Greek names. One thing we can observe is that Nicolas, a non-Jewish believer from Antioch, was chosen which indicates a crossing of cultural lines. The problem that had caused the original murmuring and division is not mentioned again. Apparently, selecting good leaders settled this issue.

How did Paul deal with the problem in Corinth?

Paul used wise teaching to encourage a new perspective in the Corinthian church. Paul wanted the Corinthians to see the big picture—various ministries within the church function together. He challenged them to look beyond their leaders to see that God brings growth to the Church.

How did Paul identify those within the church who let quarreling about leadership separate them?

Paul was very plain in identifying people who separate because of cultural differences as being "carnal" (KJV) or "worldly" (NIV) in 1 Corinthians 3:1. Strong leadership and wise teaching are given to the Church to help believers respond maturely, rather than carnally, in conflicts which might arise from cultural diversity.

Continuing in Christian Unity

In his letters to other churches, Paul frequently emphasized the importance of continuing in Christian unity. He wrote to the Galatians about racial, social, and gender equality in Christ: "There is neither Jew nor Greek, slave nor free, male nor female, for you are all one in Christ Jesus" (Galatians 3:28).

He reminded the Ephesians that Gentiles and Jews were united in Christ. The wall of separation that once divided them was destroyed by His death (Ephesians 2:11–13). Though we have that unity in Christ positionally, we need to continue our effort to see that unity is maintained. Paul understood this and challenged the Ephesians to "make every effort to keep the unity of the Spirit through the bond of peace" (Ephesians 4:3). When we embrace our cultural differences instead of letting them separate us, we are following the Scripture's instruction.

Emissaries from Chloe, a woman living in Corinth, went to Paul, describing the division in the Corinthian church. Chloe was concerned enough about the situation to do what she could to bring peace.

REFLECTING HIS IMAGE
Chloe (1 Corinthians 1:10,11)

Chloe was a woman in a dilemma. And she was tense. Very tense. Moments before, visitors dropped in unexpectedly. Ten visitors to be exact. They were friends of hers who lately couldn't seem to agree on much of anything.

She inwardly wrestled with herself as she instructed her servants to attend to her guests' needs. It wasn't as if her home was small or her pantry was empty. Chloe was a well-to-do businesswoman. But, she was nervous. Irritated! And her thoughts were occupied with the drama in the Corinthian church over the past few days.

Now, as she looked around the room into the faces of friends whose relationships were upset by constant bickering and jealousy, the uppermost question in her mind was, *What can I do to stop this backbiting?* She was disturbed by how unhappy and uneasy they looked.

Well, Chloe thought decidedly, *if they have come here—to my home, to my table—thinking I will join in or take sides, they are mistaken.*

Never mind that most of her company previously had reputations as unruly, heavy-drinking, sexually perverse people. *Those days are behind now, aren't they? Have we learned nothing from the eighteen months Paul spent with us, sharing the good news of Jesus and showing us how to live as a holy community of believers?* she wondered.

In her church, comprised of both Jews and Gentiles, serious problems needed to be addressed—all springing from an ever-growing division of mind and thought.

As Chloe pondered in her heart the conversation swirling around, her frustration turned to desperation and she prayed silently for guidance. Hours later as she said good-bye to the last of her guests, she knew what she had to do.

That evening, by lamplight, she began:

Dear Brother Paul,

Grace to you from God, our Father, and the Lord Jesus Christ, who comforts us in all our troubles.

It grieves me to report to you that there are divisions among the believers here in Corinth. We are no longer unified in mind and thought as you taught us to be. As a matter of fact, I am aware—firsthand—of misunderstandings concerning Christian beliefs, sexual misconduct, and the abuse of spiritual gifts among some of the Corinthian believers.

In addition, quarrels and backbiting have escalated to the point that some are saying, "I follow Paul," while others say, "I follow Apollos," and others say, "I follow Christ."

As I write, I am reminded of your teaching that sin is not new to the Church. You know that many of us, as new believers, come from pagan backgrounds. Idol worship and loose living were regular parts of our lives. Thanks be to God, He has not left us in our condition, but has given us new life through His Holy Spirit.

I know that all wisdom ultimately comes from God, and I would ask that you—Paul, called to be an apostle of Christ Jesus by the will of God—would help us please! We long to listen to you and learn how to live.

I am sending this letter to you by my messenger, Stephanus, and will eagerly await your reply.

Peace to you.

Most humbly,

Chloe

EMBRACING THE PENTECOSTAL PERSPECTIVE
What is the Holy Spirit teaching me?

Chloe models an excellent approach to diversity, both with her recognition of the danger of disunity and with her proactive letter writing. The New Testament world was a microcosm of today's global reality. Like modern-day cities, the streets of Corinth teemed with people from many countries. Ignoring cultural differences would have hindered the spread of the gospel, but dividing over them would have caused even more harm.

We ought to share Chloe's compelling desire to change the situation. Cultural diversity should be embraced and allowed to strengthen our lives. For this to happen, we must first find common ground, as Chloe did when she recalled the sinful past and redeemed present each of her guests had in common. Next, as the Acts 6 story relates, we can value differences by inviting the full participation of every community member. As long as the priorities of the Great Commission are kept front and center (preach the Word, pray, be filled with the Spirit), the Church can be strengthened and God's mission furthered.

What do all people have in common?

Why must we distinguish between cultural and spiritual diversity?

Identify various cultures within your community. How have you made an effort to learn more about and reach out to these cultures?

Growing up, were you the kid that was called "Four Eyes" because you wore glasses? The one calling the name? Or the worried bystander, wondering why everyone can't all get along? Let's hope you no longer identify with any of these. If you are a believer, then you are called to infiltrate this world with the light of the gospel. This means not playing the victim, labeling groups without appreciating differences, or acting as a dispassionate observer.

How do you respond in the presence of people speaking a language you do not know or dressing in their native fashions?

How can you overcome fear or discomfort in the presence of people from other cultures?

A peculiar arrogance exists in the egocentric mind-set that insists, "If you're not like me, you're wrong." Christians, in particular, must be cautious to distinguish between their nationality and their spirituality. Some have mistakenly intertwined patriotism with Christianity, creating an ineffective and offensive so-called gospel. While serving Christ can and should complement our citizenship, it should never be compromised by or subjected to political identity or any other human invention. The Spirit strives to keep us focused on the simplicity and power of Christ's gospel.

How have you seen Christianity identified with national interests? When is this healthy or unhealthy?

How does an understanding of the believer's citizenship in heaven affect her ability to embrace different cultures?

Review the outpouring of the Holy Spirit on the Day of Pentecost (Acts 2). How did cultural diversity affect that event? How can we emulate the disciples' actions today?

INVITING GOD TO CHANGE MY VIEW
What change is God asking me to make?

"I'm going in!" The woman driving the personal watercraft glanced over her shoulder in time to see her friend fall into the lake. The first time it was funny, but the third time? Not so much. As the two bickered over the reason, a distinct difference of opinion emerged. The driver insisted the passenger didn't know how to hang on, while the rider was sure poor driving was to blame.

Their interpretations are very typical and very human. We tend to place blame for unwelcome life occurrences outside ourselves. Rather than identifying with one another, we separate ourselves, easily prioritizing our opinions and preferences as superior to others. Though a generalization, this principle applies to cultural relations as well. We're more willing to appreciate food shared across borders than other commodities, and we need to take intentional steps to move toward people of different cultures.

Thankfully, God showed us how. Though the only wrongdoing in the relationship between divinity and humanity was clearly on our side, He took the first step. When Christ left heaven to embark on His earthly journey, it was the greatest cross-cultural outreach ever accomplished. The results were worth it. Now He asks us to take the first step toward people who may look and sound very different from us. And He promises it will be worth it.

Do you harbor un-Christlike prejudices? Do you need God to open your eyes to multicultural opportunities around you? Are you afraid to speak to someone of a different nationality? Do you need to repent of placing national interests before or in place of God's will? Would you like to be used to reach others in your community?

Prayer

Father, I must admit the diversity of this world is a bit intimidating. I know You have called me to love my neighbor and Your Spirit births that love in my heart. But I also know fear has taken control more than once and turned me back toward what is familiar. I pray for the boldness and love of Your Holy Spirit to lead and guide me into meaningful interaction with every member of my community. Use me to bring the light of Jesus Christ to each one. In Jesus' name, Amen.

JOURNALING

Take a few minutes to record your personal insights from the lesson.

Her Encounter with the Occult

CATCHING SIGHT
Introduction

PEOPLE ARE FASCINATED by horoscopes, fortune-telling, witchcraft, and bizarre cults. Often, their interest comes from a desire to know and control the future. Many books, television shows, and games emphasize séances, mediums, and other occult practices. As Christians, we shouldn't let a desire to know the future or a belief that superstitions are harmless lead us into condoning occult practices.

One afternoon, a Chicago bus was brimming with dozing office workers, restless punkers, and affluent shoppers. At the Clark and Webster stop, two men and a woman climbed aboard. The driver, a seasoned veteran, immediately bellowed, "Everybody watch your valuables. There are pickpockets on board."

Women clutched their purses tightly. Men put their hands on their wallets. All eyes fixed on the trio, who, looking insulted and harassed, didn't break stride as they promptly exited through the middle doors. That bus driver was vigilant in protecting his passengers.[1]

The Bible warns us to be vigilant because evil is less likely to overtake us when we're watching out for it. We should avoid any curiosity about or involvement with demonic forces or the occult. The devil is like a chained dog. He is powerless to harm us when we are outside his reach but once we enter his circle we expose ourselves to injury.

[1]Craig Brian Larson, ed., *Illustrations for Preaching and Teaching: From Leadership Journal* (Grand Rapids: Baker Books, 1993), 274.

GETTING FOCUSED

Begin your study by considering the following:

Are you able to recognize the enemy? If so, how do you respond to his tactics?

BIBLE READING

Acts 8:9–24; 13:10

New International Version

8:9 Now for some time a man named Simon had practiced sorcery in the city and amazed all the people of Samaria. He boasted that he was someone great, 10 and all the people, both high and low, gave him their attention and exclaimed, "This man is the divine power known as the Great Power." 11 They followed him because he had amazed them for a long time with his magic. 12 But when they believed Philip as he preached the good news of the kingdom of God and the name of Jesus Christ, they were baptized, both men and women. 13 Simon himself believed and was baptized. And he followed Philip everywhere, astonished by the great signs and miracles he saw.

14 When the apostles in Jerusalem heard that Samaria had accepted the word of God, they sent Peter and John to them. 15 When they arrived, they prayed for them that they might receive the Holy Spirit, 16 because the Holy Spirit had not yet come upon any of them; they had simply been baptized into the name of the Lord Jesus. 17 Then

New Living Translation

8:9 A man named Simon had been a sorcerer there for many years, claiming to be someone great. 10 The Samaritan people, from the least to the greatest, often spoke of him as "the Great One—the Power of God." 11 He was very influential because of the magic he performed. 12 But now the people believed Philip's message of Good News concerning the Kingdom of God and the name of Jesus Christ. As a result, many men and women were baptized. 13 Then Simon himself believed and was baptized. He began following Philip wherever he went, and he was amazed by the great miracles and signs Philip performed.

14 When the apostles back in Jerusalem heard that the people of Samaria had accepted God's message, they sent Peter and John there. 15 As soon as they arrived, they prayed for these new Christians to receive the Holy Spirit. 16 The Holy Spirit had not yet come upon any of them, for they had only been baptized in the name of the Lord Jesus. 17 Then Peter and John laid their

New International Version

Peter and John placed their hands on them, and they received the Holy Spirit.

18 When Simon saw that the Spirit was given at the laying on of the apostles' hands, he offered them money 19 and said, "Give me also this ability so that everyone on whom I lay my hands may receive the Holy Spirit."

20 Peter answered: "May your money perish with you, because you thought you could buy the gift of God with money! 21 You have no part or share in this ministry, because your heart is not right before God. 22 Repent of this wickedness and pray to the Lord. Perhaps he will forgive you for having such a thought in your heart. 23 For I see that you are full of bitterness and captive to sin."

24 Then Simon answered, "Pray to the Lord for me so that nothing you have said may happen to me."

13:10 "You are a child of the devil and an enemy of everything that is right! You are full of all kinds of deceit and trickery. Will you never stop perverting the right ways of the Lord?"

New Living Translation

hands upon these believers, and they received the Holy Spirit.

18 When Simon saw that the Holy Spirit was given when the apostles placed their hands upon people's heads, he offered money to buy this power. 19 "Let me have this power, too," he exclaimed, "so that when I lay my hands on people, they will receive the Holy Spirit!"

20 But Peter replied, "May your money perish with you for thinking God's gift can be bought! 21 You can have no part in this, for your heart is not right before God. 22 Turn from your wickedness and pray to the Lord. Perhaps he will forgive your evil thoughts, 23 for I can see that you are full of bitterness and held captive by sin."

24 "Pray to the Lord for me," Simon exclaimed, "that these terrible things won't happen to me!"

13:10 "You son of the Devil, full of every sort of trickery and villainy, enemy of all that is good, will you never stop perverting the true ways of the Lord?"

GAINING BIBLICAL INSIGHT
Recognizing the enemy

When the Old Testament Law was given on Mount Sinai, the first commandment emphasized the importance of placing God first in our lives. The second commandment reinforced the first, going further by forbidding the worship of images or objects. Jesus summarized the Law in two commandments: Loving God with our whole being and loving other people as we love ourselves.

In spite of the teaching of the Law, rampant idolatry in the Old Testament brought repeated judgment to Israel. Idol worship opened the door to occult practices that were vehemently condemned by the Law and punishable by death.

In the New Testament, the Early Church encountered opposition from people who practiced the occult and had many followers on more than one occasion.

In the Western world today, the occult (including witchcraft, fortune-telling with tarot cards, Satan worship, and astrology) continues to have many followers. Some activities may seem innocent or even novel, such as reading palms or tea leaves, crystal-ball gazing or playing with Ouija boards, but believers must be aware of the many forms of our enemy's attack and know how to cope with them.

An Early Encounter with the Occult

Persecution and martyrdom scattered the Jerusalem believers throughout Judea and Samaria. Wherever they went, they preached the gospel in accordance with the command of Jesus. Philip, one of the first deacons, began preaching in Samaria with miraculous results of healing and deliverance from demonic spirits.

The extraordinary events got the attention of Simon, a man who had made claims of having supernatural powers.

What was the source of Simon's power?

Who received the glory for his works and why did people fol-low him?

Simon's practices of sorcery and magic were forbidden by the Old Testament Law (Leviticus 19 through 20), yet in Samaria he practiced freely and had the acclaim of the citizenship. This shows how far people were from observing God's Law. Yet their willingness to follow a self-acclaimed pseudoreligious leader showed their hunger for the supernatural power only God possesses.

The Triumph of the Gospel

Philip came to Samaria preaching the gospel of the kingdom of God. He told the good news of Jesus' death and resurrection. His preaching was accompanied by miraculous evidences of God's power at work. People believed the Word of God as preached by Philip and expressed their belief by being baptized.

What differences do you think the people would have recog-nized between the miraculous signs that followed Philip's preaching and the works they had seen Simon do?

The preaching of the gospel and the miracles that accompanied it must have had a ring of truth that Simon's magic did not have. In fact, Simon was so impressed by the miracles and signs following Philip's ministry that the Scripture says he also believed and was baptized. Powerful preaching of the gospel and God's confirmation of His Word with signs following will turn people from occult practices to serve the living God.

The Power of the Spirit

The apostles Peter and John came to Samaria to join Philip in the revival during which so many conversions and miracles had taken place. Many people also received the Holy Spirit when the apostles prayed for them.

Simon was so impressed that he wanted the power the apostles had and offered money to try to buy that power.

What do you think Simon saw that he had not seen before?

Simon had seen miracles, healings, and great joy in the city as people were converted in response to the gospel. While this chapter does not say the believers spoke in tongues, something happened that had not previously happened, which caused Simon to offer money to be able to do what the apostles had done. Most likely, the people spoke praises in tongues, the same phenomena which had occurred in Jerusalem and later would occur at Cornelius's household and in Ephesus.

In response to Simon's offer of money, Peter called for him to show true repentance (suggesting that his former confession was only an outward show). Only true repentance—a complete turning to Christ from a life of sinfulness—can bring total deliverance from Satan's powers. Simon responded by asking Peter to pray for him so that he would find forgiveness.

We do not know whether Simon truly repented, but we do know these people in Samaria who once were carried away with the occult were now Spirit-filled believers. The Word and the Spirit overcame their interest in sorcery.

Paul's Encounter with the Occult

This was not the only encounter with the occult in the New Testament Church. Paul had at least two other encounters with sorcerers in his ministry with similar results. In Cyprus, Elymas, a sorcerer, tried to turn one of Saul's converts from the faith (Paul was also called Saul). Paul's denouncement of Elymas included many of the reasons Christians believe all forms of the occult are wrong.

Read Acts 13:10. List four phrases Paul used to describe what was wrong with Elymas.

Paul recognized the source of Elymas's power—the devil. He recognized his position—an enemy of everything right. He revealed his deceitful character and his treacherous purpose of perverting the ways of the Lord.

Paul's denouncement summarized the reasons Christians avoid anything associated with occult practice, however innocent things might seem on the surface. Instead, Christians should emulate the Samaritans and hunger for the Word and the Spirit to overcome the power and influence of Satan in their lives. Then they can live Jesus' commandments to love God supremely and others unconditionally.

Christ's power can deliver anyone involved in any kind of satanic worship or practice. Mary Magdalene's testimony of deliverance from seven devils tells us of His power. Let's look at this fictional account of how Mary Magdalene's deliverance might have occurred.

REFLECTING HIS IMAGE
Mary Magdalene (Mark 16:9)

She sat outside the gate digging in the dirt with her hands, then spinning around and around in circles like a dog chasing its tail. A passerby whispered to her companion, "Don't look at her; it only makes it worse. She's not right in the head. Just ignore her."

The woman by the gate was young, twenty-something, although her leathery skin told a different story. Her piercing voice, matted hair, and mismatched clothes were unwelcome in any crowd, and today was no exception.

"Not the same, not the same, not the same," she fumed as she began to draw odd shapes in the dirt, all the while drooling and pulling at her hair.

Others in her village continued to pass her by and, while they felt great pity for her, they also felt uncomfortable, scared even. *Is she dangerous? What else might she do or say? Should we help her? Chain her? Ignore her altogether?*

Such was the life of the village madwoman known as Mary of Magdala. Day after day, she was spat upon, ridiculed, pitied, mocked, and held at arm's length.

That is, by everyone but Him.

The afternoon heat was stifling as Jesus and His disciples made their way toward the town. Hungry and weary, one of the men set out to buy provisions for their evening meal while the others found the cool of a shade tree. Jesus sat down with His disciples and began to teach.

Before long, a crowd gathered to hear this Man who spoke with knowledge and authority. Suddenly, Mary appeared in the circle and bellowed with a loud deep cry. "Not the same, not the same. I know You, I know You," she cried over and over again. "Holy One, Son of God, Holy One, Son of God."

Without warning, she rose up on her toes. Hissing like a snake and with eyes like fire, she lunged forward, striking one of the disciples with her clawlike hands.

Jesus stood and spoke. "Come out of her!" He said sternly to the demon, and the demon left her.

Instantly, another demon threw Mary to the ground. "I curse You, Son of God. I curse You, Master, Redeemer," the demon bellowed.

Again, Jesus drove out the spirit. "Leave her!" He commanded. The demon fled.

The crowd watched in bewilderment and wonder as a total of seven demons were cast from Mary the madwoman that day. Finally, as she lay helpless, exhausted, and exposed to the crowd, she looked up to see a Man standing beside her. Gently, Jesus stretched out His hand to help her to her feet.

Now, aware of her surroundings and the stares of the townspeople, she brushed her hair from her face and began to straighten her clothes as the others looked on. *Who is this Man?* Mary wondered.

A hush fell on the circle of townspeople, and without saying a word, she bowed her head in humble adoration of this Man whose very presence brought the peace to her mind and body she had never known before. She was changed—no longer a madwoman. Jesus brought deliverance. She was whole, changed, not the same. No. Certainly not the same.

EMBRACING THE PENTECOSTAL PERSPECTIVE
What is the Holy Spirit teaching me?

Every believer shares Mary's three-word testimony: "Not the same." The succinct statement speaks volumes. Knowing Jesus changes everything. Inviting Him to be your Lord and Savior places a serious line of demarcation across the record of your life, declaring every bad thing that came before as distinctly past. Everything that lies ahead can be different through the power of the Holy Spirit.

The line also marks the boundary between the kingdoms of darkness and light. Many Christians do not believe Satan exists, let alone believe he has anything to do with them. Beyond the dismal statement this makes about their deficient understanding of God's Word and doctrine, not believing in Satan's existence places many believers in a precarious position. The enemy is very real, and the evidence of his doomed, yet active, kingdom abounds.

Saturday morning cartoons have become blatantly occultic. Television programming, which often reflects popular interests, has moved through most of its overt fascination with the occult to more sophisticated forms. Christians who let down their defenses toward these accepted trends run the risk of susceptibility and worse, an inability to recognize and confront evil.

Where have you observed occultic influence in society?

What does spiritual carelessness look like?

Sometimes people are not careless intentionally but rather by sheer ignorance. **What do all Christians need to know about the enemy, his kingdom, and their relationship to it through Jesus Christ?**

We do not have the luxury or choice of indifference to the work of the enemy. For the sake of personal spiritual health—and that of the world to which we are called to deliver light—we must exercise the spiritual gifts of discernment made available through the Holy Spirit.

Is it wrong to dabble in the occult (e.g., read your horoscope, consult a fortune-teller, etc.)? Why or why not?

How can you increase your spiritual discernment?

Most women have an aversion to killing insects of any kind. One woman recalls that during her childhood, she called on her parents frequently to kill insects on her behalf. Eventually, her parents began to ignore her whining pleas for help and insisted that the girl handle her own exterminations. The girl slept with a sheet over her head or moved to another room to avoid any crawling intruders. Later, as she began living on her own, circumstances and desperation forced the girl to eliminate her first moth. Totally grossed out, but surprisingly satisfied, she shared her tale of victory with her friends. Given the fact that the girl outweighed the enemy by an exponential factor, the friends were unimpressed.

"The one who is in you is greater than the one who is in the world" (1 John 4:4). Do you believe it? How should this promise shape your attitude toward the enemy?

Knowing the power of Jesus that abides in you through His Spirit, how would you confront a demonic situation?

INVITING GOD TO CHANGE MY VIEW
What change is God asking me to make?

"You're scared, aren't you?" the woman said. With the emergency counseling session approaching its third hour, the pastor was many things—weary, concerned, hungry (it was past lunchtime!), and way down deep, yes, scared. Not about to admit such a thing to a person whom she was certain entertained the occult, the pastor continued to pray fervently and speak God's Word authoritatively.

After the woman left, the pastor was still shaken by the experience. Like most believers, there were countless Bible stories in which she had pictured herself as a chief character. A dressed-down version of the sons of Sceva was not one of them (Acts 19:14). Fear is a palpable thing, and in that moment everyone—pastor, parishioner, and evil spirit—recognized it. The pastor determined that never again would fear, or the spiritual condition that cultivated it, be permitted. Recognizing the enemy? No problem. But when the enemy recognizes you, instead of Jesus, whose righteousness is supposed to clothe you? Big problem.

Do you need to grow in discernment? Do you value and desire spiritual perception over naiveté? Does fear occupy your heart with regard to the occult? Are you praying and fasting faithfully? Do you pray in the Spirit regularly? Do you know how to confront the enemy once you have recognized him? Do you need to understand the power and authority of Jesus' name and righteousness?

Prayer

Thank you, Jesus, for overcoming the enemy of our souls! Long ago, You won the victory over every opposing spirit. Remind me that the victory applies today. Sometimes, it seems the enemy is winning, and I shut my eyes to the reality of what is going on around me. But I know that neither of these responses reflects the power of Your Spirit in me. Open my eyes, Lord. Give me the gift of discernment through Your Holy Spirit. I cannot afford to ignore the battle. Guard me from the fear and panic of a conspiracy mindset and make me know the truth. For Yours is the Kingdom, and the power, and the glory forever! Amen.

JOURNALING

Take a few minutes to record your personal insights from the lesson.

Her Sexual Ethics

CATCHING SIGHT
Introduction

*O*UR NATION'S ETHICS have reached an all-time low, while sexual promiscuity has reached an all-time high. Unmarried couples cohabitate as husband and wife, and an alarming degree of sexual activity exists among teens and even children. Elected officials openly engage in adulterous relationships, and sports figures who boast of their sexual indiscretions are seen as heroes. Years ago, a person had to go out of his or her way to find pornography—but not anymore. Pornography is available in movie theaters, at video stores, and on television, and is dangerously accessible through the Internet.

The Old and New Testaments include warnings of judgment and punishment for the sin of homosexuality. Yet our children are taught that homosexuality is merely an alternate lifestyle. They are pressured to tolerate the very practice for which God destroyed Sodom and Gomorrah.

With loose morals comes a particularly destructive disease—the loss of true love for God and others. Sin has a way of cooling our love for God and others by turning our focus on ourselves. Self-gratification is high on the list of priorities for most people today. Two of the most difficult sins to resist are pride and sexual immorality. Both are seductive. Pride says, "I deserve it," while sexual immorality says, "I need it." In combination, their appeal is deadly.

GETTING FOCUSED

Begin your study by considering the following:

How can we honor God and have strong sexual ethics in this pleasure-seeking world?

BIBLE READING

1 Corinthians 5:1–5; 6:12–20

New International Version

5:1 It is actually reported that there is sexual immorality among you, and of a kind that does not occur even among pagans: A man has his father's wife. 2 And you are proud! Shouldn't you rather have been filled with grief and have put out of your fellowship the man who did this? 3 Even though I am not physically present, I am with you in spirit. And I have already passed judgment on the one who did this, just as if I were present. 4 When you are assembled in the name of our Lord Jesus and I am with you in spirit, and the power of our Lord Jesus is present, 5 hand this man over to Satan, so that the sinful nature may be destroyed and his spirit saved on the day of the Lord.

6:12 "Everything is permissible for me"—but not everything is beneficial. "Everything is permissible for me"—but I will not be mastered by anything. 13 "Food for the stomach and the stomach for food"—but God will destroy them both. The body is not meant for sexual immorality, but for the Lord, and the Lord

New Living Translation

5:1 I can hardly believe the report about the sexual immorality going on among you, something so evil that even the pagans don't do it. I am told that you have a man in your church who is living in sin with his father's wife. 2 And you are so proud of yourselves! Why aren't you mourning in sorrow and shame? And why haven't you removed this man from your fellowship?

3 Even though I am not there with you in person, I am with you in the Spirit. Concerning the one who has done this, I have already passed judgment 4 in the name of the Lord Jesus. You are to call a meeting of the church, and I will be there in spirit, and the power of the Lord Jesus will be with you as you meet. 5 Then you must cast this man out of the church and into Satan's hands, so that his sinful nature will be destroyed and he himself will be saved when the Lord returns.

6:12 You may say, "I am allowed to do anything." But I reply, "Not everything is good for you." And even though "I am allowed to do

New International Version

for the body. 14 By his power God raised the Lord from the dead, and he will raise us also. 15 Do you not know that your bodies are members of Christ himself? Shall I then take the members of Christ and unite them with a prostitute? Never! 16 Do you not know that he who unites himself with a prostitute is one with her in body? For it is said, "The two will become one flesh." 17 But he who unites himself with the Lord is one with him in spirit.

18 Flee from sexual immorality. All other sins a man commits are outside his body, but he who sins sexually sins against his own body. 19 Do you not know that your body is a temple of the Holy Spirit, who is in you, whom you have received from God? You are not your own; 20 you were bought at a price. Therefore honor God with your body.

New Living Translation

anything," I must not become a slave to anything. 13 You say, "Food is for the stomach, and the stomach is for food." This is true, though someday God will do away with both of them. But our bodies were not made for sexual immorality. They were made for the Lord, and the Lord cares about our bodies. 14 And God will raise our bodies from the dead by his marvelous power, just as he raised our Lord from the dead.

15 Don't you realize that your bodies are actually parts of Christ? Should a man take his body, which belongs to Christ, and join it to a prostitute? Never! 16 And don't you know that if a man joins himself to a prostitute, he becomes one body with her? For the Scriptures say, "The two are united into one." 17 But the person who is joined to the Lord becomes one spirit with him.

18 Run away from sexual sin! No other sin so clearly affects the body as this one does. For sexual immorality is a sin against your own body. 19 Or don't you know that your body is the temple of the Holy Spirit, who lives in you and was given to you by God? You do not belong to yourself, 20 for God bought you with a high price. So you must honor God with your body.

GAINING BIBLICAL INSIGHT
Honoring God with integrity

The Bible introduces human sexuality in its opening chapter. Two distinct genders were part of God's creation, which He declared to be "very good." Genesis 2 reveals His design for the intergender relationship, including union, companionship, and procreation. Unfolding biblical revelation includes instructions for healthy sexual relationships within marriage and warnings against all kinds of illicit sex.

This relationship between the sexes is so vital it serves as a metaphor for the relationship between God and humankind. The tender love relationship between a husband and wife illustrates the Old Testament love of God for Israel and the New Testament love of Christ for the Church. When the nation of Israel turned its back on God, He called it an adulterous nation.

Throughout history, people have distorted God's original plan for sexuality by ignoring His Word. In the twenty-first century, we find ourselves in a hedonistic culture obsessed with unrestricted sex. Yet Christians still look to the Bible to understand God's design for beautiful, wholesome sexual relationships.

Recognizing Sexual Sin

Illicit sexual relationships were a problem even in the Early Church. Paul described a situation of sexual immorality which the church in Corinth had ignored. Paul, however, recognized the sexual relationship for what it was—sin.

If we want to understand biblical sexuality, we first must understand some foundational biblical principles given to help us to recognize sinful relationships. Some people assume that sex itself is sinful. However, this cannot be true because the distinct genders were created by God and He gave instructions for their relationship. The *violation* of God's design is sinful. In our example, a Corinthian man had entered a sexual relationship with his stepmother, a blatant violation of God's plan. Amazingly, the church was not bothered by this incestuous relationship. In fact, they seemed to be encouraging it.

Why do you think the Corinthian church overlooked this glaring sin?

The church may have been motivated by a distorted sense of grace and love. Sometimes, Christians emphasize God's love to the point of minimizing His holiness. When repentance happens, grace covers sin. God's love reaches to sinners so they might be delivered from their sin, not continue in it.

Sometimes, Christians are reluctant to deal with sin because they don't want to appear judgmental. But Paul did not hesitate to pass judgment on this situation which was blatantly in violation of known principles of righteous living. This person had gone far beyond Jesus' teaching that even lustful thoughts were adulterous (Matthew 5:27–29). The sin needed to be recognized for what it was and dealt with accordingly.

Dealing with Sexual Sin

Spiritual well-being is always a reason to deal with sin in our own lives or confront it in others. Sin impairs spiritual growth and will ultimately destroy the person who continues sinning.

Paul encouraged the Corinthian church to deal immediately with this sinful situation. Although Paul's advice was direct to the point of being harsh, we understand he had the ultimate good of the man—and the church—in mind.

What was Paul's long-term goal for the man according to 1 Corinthians 5:5?

The man's eternal salvation was of utmost importance to Paul. Later, Paul revealed his compassion when he wrote to the Corinthians again, encouraging them to accept a restored sinner (2 Corinthians 2:5–11). Some scholars think he was referring to the restoration of the same man.

Paul had another reason for dealing with this sin—the health of the body of Christ (1 Corinthians 5:6–13). He draws an illustration from the Jewish custom of ridding houses of all yeast before the Passover as a symbol of removing sin from their lives. Similarly, believers must remove sin from their midst so they can worship in "sincerity and truth" (verse 8).

Understanding Sexual Integrity

In dealing with this one sexual sin, Paul gave us guidelines for understanding the importance of sexual integrity as a means of honoring God. We see our bodies not as our own to be used for our own self-indulgent pleasure, but as a means of bringing glory to God.

Apparently, in Corinth the teaching of freedom in Christ had gone so far that some were saying, "Everything is permissible to me." The Corinthians implied that, since God created sexual drives, He must have wanted people to have the freedom to gratify their drives, and the sex act was for the body what food was for the stomach. They considered sex to be only a physical act with no bearing on spirituality.

Paul demonstrated the fallacy of this argument by turning their thoughts from what is *permissible* to what is *beneficial*. While it might be physically possible to turn the body into a sex machine, Paul wanted them to see a higher purpose for their bodies. He specifically stated that the body was not created for sexual immorality. God had other plans.

Paul gave the Corinthians three reasons for maintaining sexual purity, each reason relating to a member of the Trinity. He first wanted them to respect their bodies as members of Christ's body. He talked about two very different kinds of unity here—unity with Christ or illicit sexual unity. In sexual intercourse, two people are physically united for life, whether this act happens in the legitimate framework of marriage or otherwise. Paul pleaded with the Christians to remember their unity with Christ and to avoid illicit sexual union.

He employed another metaphor by comparing the body to a temple in which the Holy Spirit dwells. All kinds of sexual immorality are sins against the body which God created for higher purposes. The body should be cared for just as we would care for the finest temple because it is the place where the Holy Spirit abides.

Paul's final plea for avoiding sexual immorality was for the Corinthians to honor God with their bodies. When you are a Christian, your body belongs to God. It is given to you as a means of honoring Him.

The Bible tells of a woman in a pagan culture who respected her body so much that she would not parade it before a group of drunken men. Vashti's refusal cost her a great deal, but we remember her for her courageous stand.

REFLECTING HIS IMAGE
Vashti (Esther 1)

The wine had flowed freely in King Xerxes's banquet hall for the past several days, as dignitaries in Susa, the capital of Persia, gathered for a weeklong party where no expense was spared. The king's cool, dark eyes took in the adulation he craved as he displayed his vast wealth and power. But he had saved his most lovely possession for last.

Elsewhere in the lavish palace, Queen Vashti sighed and stared blankly into space as her maids attended to her hair.

What is he thinking? she asked herself, angry at the thought of being summoned and paraded in front of drunken men as the "grand finale" for her husband's impressive banquet. *If he were sober enough to think clearly, he would not ask me to make such an appearance. He knows full well that Persian custom dictates I remain in seclusion during occasions like this.*

Dismissing her servants, the queen stood erect and passed slowly through the white and violet linen curtains to the outer porch. She had a decision to make and she needed time to be alone—to think. A Persian princess by birth, Vashti was proud and possessed an undeniably regal beauty and bearing which corresponded to the meaning of her name: "beautiful woman."

But she was also a woman of integrity. And the thought of appearing as nothing more than a prized trophy in the king's banquet hall, in her royal robes and crown before a wine-soaked audience, made her blood run cold. *What of my dignity and honor?* she wondered.

Knowing what her refusal could mean, she hesitated—but only briefly. "Let this crowd feast their eyes on the king's other wives," she whispered softly, resolutely, to herself. "I will not go."

The news of her decision traveled quickly to the enclosed garden of the palace, where an intoxicated King Xerxes shook his head incredulously. "How dare the queen refuse to come at my command!" he shouted. "How dare she humiliate me like this!"

Flanked by his advisors, he immediately took action.

"The Queen has not only acted against you, but against all the people and officials in every province. Save face," they said. "Banishment and divorce are the only fit punishments for her disrespect."

Weeks later—relieved and again alone in her thoughts—Vashti, stripped of the life and luxury she had known, smiled to herself. Satisfied that she had chosen honor rather than dishonor, she had given up her crown to preserve her dignity. But she had never felt more like a queen.

EMBRACING THE PENTECOSTAL PERSPECTIVE
What is the Holy Spirit teaching me?

Our circumstances most likely pale in comparison to Queen Vashti's life-changing situation. Or do they? Though the idea of being commanded to do such a thing seems fairly remote, the consequences of her choice strike uncomfortably close. Every day, we can choose to live lives of integrity in the power of the Spirit. But every time we choose poorly, in a way that disgraces our King, we divorce ourselves from Kingdom life. For Vashti, standing separate from Xerxes's worldly character was an excellent choice. But for Christians, standing in opposition to Christ's call to holiness divorces us from His goodness—a poor choice, indeed.

Actions, including those pertaining to sex, should be guided by a character shaped by God's Spirit. Sinful actions result from temptation that has come full-term. The believer must recognize temptation quickly and act accordingly to either flee or kill it before the temptation can give birth to sin. Resisting sexual temptation, which is particularly powerful, requires responsiveness that results from understanding God's Word, biblical standards for purity, and intentional safeguards and accountability.

What causes the most sexual temptation for you—television, the Internet, conversations with coworkers, or something else? How do you protect against such temptations?

Why does the world insist on conforming Christ to its sexually deviant image (e.g., fabricating a relationship with Mary Magdelene in fictitious accounts such as *The DaVinci Code*)?

The subject of sexuality is a minefield full of false information. Thanks to the uninformed tales of schoolmates and an overly obsessed media, believers of all ages may find themselves in need of sex education. The Corinthians certainly were! So start with the Word of God. A "right or wrong" mentality is an inadequate way to respond to people with no other point of reference than the behavior of those around them. We must be prepared to speak the truth with grace and intelligence!

What does the Bible say about homosexuality, sex in marriage, sex outside of marriage, and celibacy (sexual abstinence/ purity)?

Knowing God's intentions and instructions only prepares us for a conversation. Integrity gives us the credibility to speak and God's truth gives us guidance. The world is a messy place, though, and we need to be ready to speak in that context. With the leading and courage of the Spirit, we can boldly engage the world.

What do you say to a coworker who wants to know if God hates homosexual people? (Don't say, "God hates the sin but loves the sinner." It is an overused, weak answer.)

How do you address a married friend who insists sexually charged Internet chat rooms are just "harmless" entertainment?

What do you say to your family member who is single and sexually promiscuous?

How do you counsel a Christian parent who naively thinks there is no reason to discuss sexual matters with her preteen?

INVITING GOD TO CHANGE MY VIEW
What change is God asking me to make?

"It wasn't supposed to be this way!" the graphic artist cried. After countless hours spent designing the print document, she could not have been more disappointed. "It didn't look this way on my computer screen. And the proofs did not show this distortion. I can't believe we are stuck with this inferior product. Can't we have it redone?" Sadly, there was no time to redo the piece. It was mailed out that afternoon—its important message diluted, if not obscured, by a product that did not match its original design and intent.

Do you wonder if God ever feels this way about His creation? He designed an unimaginably beautiful world, intricately perfect in every detail, but sin mars that plan. Even His plan for sexuality—something practical, intimate, and pleasurable—has been distorted in ways too horrible to describe. Imagine how His heart aches over this outcome!

Thankfully, Jesus restores the beauty that God intended. We, His creation, can display the wonder of His plan. Instead of mirroring the brokenness of the world, we can reflect the integrity of a life made whole through the Savior. No matter what happened in the past, the present and future can be completely redeemed through Him. That message must not be hidden or distorted. It must be heard!

You cannot be an effective believer, either personally or evangelistically, with a "bury-your-head-in-the-sand" mentality toward sex. Do you need to repent of either naiveté or ignorance with regard to sexual integrity? Do you need to repent of sexual sin? Do you need to set up accountability systems in your life? Are you afraid to speak to those close to you about their sinful habits or behaviors? Will you ask the Spirit to teach you what God has to say about human sexuality?

Prayer

Father, this is a tough subject. The world seems to have no trouble talking about sex, and yet we have avoided talking about it in the Church. I realize the danger of that, and I do not want to imitate the Corinthians who actually defended sexual sin. I pray for open eyes and a heart tuned to Yours. Empower me to recognize and resist temptation. Give me courage to speak the truth with grace. Above all, enable me to live a life of integrity, honoring Your perfect design. Amen.

JOURNALING
Take a few minutes to record your personal insights from the lesson.

Her Sense of Style

CATCHING SIGHT
Introduction

WE ARE ALWAYS communicating, whether we intend to or not. Author Lisa Bevere says, "Our messages will go out through one of three channels: *what we say* (our words and tone), *what we do* (our manners and actions), and *what we look like* (our visual appearances or presentations)."[1]

I was surprised when my second-grader announced that he didn't have nice clothes like his friends had. He explained that all the boys were wearing shirts with tiny alligators—a famous label icon—on the chest. He was already choosing his style according to what his friends were wearing. When I checked on the cost of such shirts, I discovered they cost at least twice what I normally paid for his shirts. The dilemma was solved by purchasing a pair of alligator socks, removing the alligators, and sewing them on several of his shirts. My son thought he had been raised to another social level. But by third grade, his sense of style had changed again and alligator shirts were no longer important.

You may be thinking, *Appearance shouldn't matter because God looks at the heart.* True, but we still live on earth. Modesty, or the lack thereof, is a major issue because people are often more influenced by what they see than by what they hear. This is truer for men than women because men are more sight-oriented and visually aware.

We can be fashionable and attractive without being molded into a worldly image. Sadly, these lines are blurred daily. It sometimes seems that Christians are no longer a counterculture but a copycat subculture.

---

[1] Lisa Bevere, *Kissed the Girls and Made Them Cry* (Nashville: Thomas Nelson, 2002),154.

GETTING FOCUSED

Begin your study by considering the following:

What styles of dress do you consider too seductive?

BIBLE READING

1 Corinthians 11:3–10; 1 Timothy 2:9,10; 1 Peter 3:3,4

New International Version

1 Corinthians 11:3 Now I want you to realize that the head of every man is Christ, and the head of the woman is man, and the head of Christ is God. 4 Every man who prays or prophesies with his head covered dishonors his head. 5 And every woman who prays or prophesies with her head uncovered dishonors her head—it is just as though her head were shaved. 6 If a woman does not cover her head, she should have her hair cut off; and if it is a disgrace for a woman to have her hair cut or shaved off, she should cover her head. 7 A man ought not to cover his head, since he is the image and glory of God; but the woman is the glory of man. 8 For man did not come from woman, but woman from man; 9 neither was man created for woman, but woman for man. 10 For this reason, and because of the angels, the woman ought to have a sign of authority on her head.

1 Timothy 2:9 I also want women to dress modestly, with decency and propriety, not with braided hair or gold or pearls or expensive clothes, 10 but with good deeds, appropriate

New Living Translation

1 Corinthians 11:3 But there is one thing I want you to know: A man is responsible to Christ, a woman is responsible to her husband, and Christ is responsible to God. 4 A man dishonors Christ if he covers his head while praying or prophesying. 5 But a woman dishonors her husband if she prays or prophesies without a covering on her head, for this is the same as shaving her head. 6 Yes, if she refuses to wear a head covering, she should cut off all her hair. And since it is shameful for a woman to have her hair cut or her head shaved, then she should wear a covering. 7 A man should not wear anything on his head when worshiping, for man is God's glory, made in God's own image, but woman is the glory of man. 8 For the first man didn't come from woman, but the first woman came from man. 9 And man was not made for woman's benefit, but woman was made for man. 10 So a woman should wear a covering on her head as a sign of authority because the angels are watching.

1 Timothy 2:9 And I want women to be modest in their appearance.

New International Version

for women who profess to worship
God.

1 Peter 3:3 Your beauty should not
come from outward adornment,
such as braided hair and the wearing
of gold jewelry and fine clothes.
4 Instead, it should be that of your
inner self, the unfading beauty of a
gentle and quiet spirit, which is of
great worth in God's sight.

New Living Translation

They should wear decent and appropriate clothing and not draw
attention to themselves by the way
they fix their hair or by wearing gold
or pearls or expensive clothes. 10 For
women who claim to be devoted to
God should make themselves attractive by the good things they do.

1 Peter 3:3 Don't be concerned
about the outward beauty that de-
pends on fancy hairstyles, expensive
jewelry, or beautiful clothes. 4 You
should be known for the beauty that
comes from within, the unfading
beauty of a gentle and quiet spirit,
which is so precious to God.

GAINING BIBLICAL INSIGHT
Sending the right message

"Your body belongs to God." Sound familiar? That's how our last
lesson ended. Truly our body belongs to God, but we face the daily
dilemma of clothing it. So many factors affect our decision: weather,
personal tastes, what we can afford, what fits, what is clean and
mended, and what plans we have for that day.

In addition, we feel pressure from constantly changing styles.
While we may not want to be a fashion trendsetter, neither do we
want to look as if we came from our grandmother's attic. No virtue
exists per se in the clothing styles of any certain era. The issue for the
Christian woman is choosing styles that reflect her understanding of
biblical values of modesty.

For Christians, another factor enters the mix—the desire to honor
God. Clothing communicates a powerful nonverbal message. Within
a few seconds of meeting someone, your appearance has revealed

your attitude toward yourself, your peers, and your culture. Dress is particularly important when you want to convey your commitment to sexual integrity.

Modesty: An Issue Relating to Our Worship

The question of appropriate dress is not new. Paul dealt with the issue when writing to the Corinthian church. Like an artist painting with bold brush strokes, Paul covered many issues in 1 Corinthians 11. However, we will discuss only one: the matter of dress as it relates to worship.

First, Paul reminded the Corinthians of the interrelatedness of men, women, and Christ (verses 3,4) and the manner that appropriately reflects that relationship during worship. Without getting into varying cultural aspects of dress, let us deal with the larger issue here. Paul was saying appearance reveals relationship, so we should ask ourselves as we come to worship, "What does my appearance say about my relationship to God?"

Some have argued that it doesn't matter how we dress for worship because God looks at the heart (1 Samuel 16:7). But the truth is, the outward appearance should accurately reflect what is within; otherwise we lack integrity because we send an unclear message by our dress.

The married woman must ask herself a second question, "What does my manner of dress say about my relationship to my husband?" Paul continued his message by saying a woman's style may show disrespect to her husband (1 Corinthians 11:5). In first-century Corinthian culture, it was disrespectful to the husband for a wife to have her head uncovered. Other cultures have other symbols of respect in the marriage relationship. The point is, a married Christian woman respects her husband and her own body by dressing discreetly, particularly when worshipping. She dresses in a manner that reflects the mutual respect she and her husband have for their sacred marriage relationship and for each other.

Modest dressing also shows respect for community values. In Corinth, the whole community knew an uncovered head was a sign of availability as a prostitute (verse 6). A shaved head could indicate that a woman had been publicly accused of prostitution or was blatantly ignoring community values by appearing as one accused of sexual sin.

A Christian woman considers the style of her clothing to see what message it is sending. Does it communicate modesty, or is it flaunting sexuality? Fashion designers attempt to accentuate a woman's sex appeal. While Christian women understand and appreciate their God-given sexuality, they should seriously weigh their decisions on style of dress.

Though this passage specifically addresses the relationship of married people and worship, the principles apply to single persons as well. Modesty of dress for any individual, single or married, who participates in public worship should reflect respect for herself as a sexual being, respect for others, and respect for the God who created each of us as we are.

Modesty: An Issue Relating to Our Daily Life

Modesty is not only an issue in worship but also in everyday relationships. In an attempt to maintain modesty, some have gone to an extreme in the other direction dressing very plainly. **What is beauty's place in a woman's wardrobe and life?**

When you look at beauty in creation, you know God loves variety, color, and style. Since God created so much beauty, He must not believe it is wrong. **In the Old Testament, many women are described as "beautiful." Take a minute to list some of them.**

Read 1 Timothy 2:9,10. Some people read this passage and think styled hair, jewelry, and beautiful clothes have no place in the life of a Christian. However, a careful reading will catch Paul's appeal for balancing beauty and good works. Key words are "modestly," "decency," and "propriety," which suggest parameters for dress.

Modesty refers to a manner of dress that does not call attention to itself. Overdone hairstyles, gaudy jewelry, and extreme clothing shouting for attention should not be the first thing people notice about a Christian woman. Her modesty should keep her from dressing this way.

Decency suggests a Christian woman's respect for herself and others and consideration for the values of her community. When current trends call for revealing styles, she chooses decency over conformity to fashion. Her manner of dress will be chaste but not frumpy.

Propriety indicates a sense of style that knows what is appropriate for the occasion. A Christian woman's discriminating taste helps her make good judgments so her life honors God.

Notice the correlation of modesty of dress and good works; neither replaces the other. A person cannot say, "Look at all the things I am doing for the Lord! What I wear doesn't matter." Neither should a person place so much emphasis on dress that a wrong attitude negates her good works.

What Paul wants is balance of beauty and good works. Beautiful deeds should be the companions of a beautiful person. The modesty practiced in worship becomes a lifestyle.

Modesty: An Issue Revealing Our Hearts

Peter joined Paul in his teaching about modesty of dress, almost reiterating the same statements (1 Peter 3:3,4). In this passage, Peter is concerned with the source and substance of beauty.

What is the source of beauty according to Peter?

He wanted women to understand beauty does not come from the outside but from the inside; it is internal, not external.

What is the substance of beauty?

A beautiful spirit is what makes a woman beautiful according to Peter. Fancy hairdos, jewelry, and fashionable clothing are not the substance of true beauty. To be truly beautiful, a woman must have a gentle and quiet spirit—traits of a modest woman.

Sarah was one woman described in the Old Testament as beautiful. What can we learn from her?

REFLECTING HIS IMAGE
Sarah (Genesis 12:1–4)

From a distance, he watched her enter the tent, confidently, stately with her maid following close behind. Today she was wearing deep emerald green, no doubt to set off her brown eyes. Her demure veil softly billowed as she walked and he realized it was the first time in a while he'd seen her carefully coiffed hair down around her shoulders.

Sarah was walking toward her husband with a determination that warmed his heart. It was just a meal and conversation together, but her entrance was all for him! *How beautiful she is*, Abraham thought. *And how blessed I am*.

Leaving their home in Ur had not been easy for Sarah, but she willingly and lovingly joined her husband as they began the busy preparations for what she suspected might be a long journey. The Lord had spoken, giving clear direction for the family to leave their country and their father's house and travel to a land yet unseen. A promise was given that God's blessing would rest upon them as a great new nation was formed.

So together they left everything familiar behind them, including friends and clan—never to return. Not knowing their destination would have been an impossible challenge for some travelers, but not for Abraham and Sarah. He was close to seventy-five years of age, and she was ten years younger, but they journeyed on, happily anticipating the promised blessings of God.

Now, as Abraham looked lovingly across the table at his wife, he marveled at how good the years had been to her. *She is still one of the most beautiful women in the land and she becomes more beautiful as time passes,* he thought. *Wherever we go, other men will admire her. Who can blame them?*

Food was scarce now and when he heard there was grain in Egypt, he decided to go there. However, compared to the dusky Egyptians, Sarah had fair skin and would attract too much attention. Fear began to gnaw at his heart and in an instant he knew what he had to do for both their sakes.

Later that evening, alone with his thoughts, he devised his plan. *Sarah's beauty is beyond compare,* he thought. *And while I know full well the power she has over me, I also know her inner beauty and strength of character. She has trusted me to lead and provide for her in the past. She will trust me now.*

EMBRACING THE PENTECOSTAL PERSPECTIVE
What is the Holy Spirit teaching me?

Sarah probably would have fit in with the "Don't-hate-me-because-I'm-beautiful" crowd who adorned a cosmetic company's marketing campaign years ago. Like Abraham, the person behind those advertisements took a big risk. Tweaking the tail of jealousy in the hopes of provoking favor makes for a dangerous game. Knowing your audience is key and the advertisers knew theirs. Women want to be beautiful.

The difficulty today, just as it was in Sarah's day and in that of the Early Church, is deciding who and what will define beauty in life. Will it be the advertisers, the cosmetic companies, the entertainment industry, and the magazines? If so, women may ignore God's Word and the voice of His Spirit and be trapped in a web of the world's making—temporary at best, dangerous at worst.

How does a typical secular woman's magazine define beauty?

What characteristics do you look for in a good friend? Do any of them concern physical appearance? What does this tell us about its relative importance?

How can you create a culture of God-defined beauty around you? (e.g., How can you affirm the beauty of godliness in others? How will you measure your own beauty?)

"Why does a twelve-year-old need a padded bra?" raged the father of a preteen girl. His indignation, though amusing to onlookers, was both righteous and necessary. No area of discipleship is more volatile than that of clothing choices. Expecting people to share a sense of what is or is not decent pushes the capacity of common sense too far. Attempts to define holiness via the closet have always proved destructive. On the other hand, adopting an "anything goes" attitude defies the truth that walking with Christ impacts our choices.

How can we teach principles of style that honor Christ to young women and new believers of any age?

A visitor arrives at your church dressed inappropriately. How should you respond? Should the response differ if the person is a longtime attendee?

Some women believe that God directs their daily choice of clothing. However, while God cares about the little things and hears and answers prayer, He also gives us clear instruction through His Word, the mind of Christ, and His Holy Spirit. Are we really so incapable of applying His instruction to the simple task of clothing ourselves? Let's move on to the more weighty matters of personal style!

How can we employ God's instruction with regard to these matters of wardrobe: budget, motivation, self-discipline, and representing Christ?

How can you give the Spirit more access to your life to continue the good work that He has begun with regard to fashioning you in the image of Christ?

INVITING GOD TO CHANGE MY VIEW
What change is God asking me to make?

Switching seasonal wardrobes seems to be the bane of many a woman's existence. Perhaps you live in a climate of year-round temperature perfection, but for many, the semiannual exchange of summer and winter clothing is a very real task.

Many women live with a severe shortage of closet space. Off-season clothing is sometimes stacked in garbage bags or kept in plastic storage containers. Each time the great seasonal swap takes place, women are amazed at how many items probably belong in the trash. What seems like a must-have item one year is often never worn the next. Though changing styles are sometimes the culprits, poor choices and size fluctuations are more often the reasons for abandonment.

Isn't the same true of the work of God's Spirit in our lives? He constantly works in us to outfit us for life in God's Kingdom. Amazing transformation occurs instantaneously when we begin walking with Christ but it is just the beginning. Like our clothing, numerous elements of our lives—when examined in the light of new life, higher purpose, and a genuine desire to please God—just do not fit. Insisting on my right to hang onto these things endangers the ongoing growth the Spirit endeavors to create.

Are you unduly obsessed with the world's standard of style? Are you troubled by a lack of certainty that God has created you uniquely and perfectly? Are you unconvinced that "God don't make no junk"? What characteristics of Christ need to be fine-tuned in your life to display the beauty of holiness? What ill-fitting garment from your past or present do you need to discard in order to grow spiritually?

Prayer

Father, I really do want to please You. I want to reflect the beauty of Your Son. I want Your glory to increase in me. I know You look on the heart, and I invite You to look at mine. Show me, by Your Spirit, what I need to let go of and what I need to focus on. Enable me to honor You with my appearance and my actions. Let our family resemblance be visible before anything else. Amen.

JOURNALING

Take a few minutes to record your personal insights from the lesson.

Her Tough Choices

CATCHING SIGHT
Introduction

I WATCH THE news in disbelief: A ten-month-old girl was accidentally locked inside a parked car on a ninety-nine-degree September day in San Antonio. Frantically, the mother ran around the car desperately searching for a way to save her baby. The reporter said that the infant was turning purple from the heat.

When a nearby truck driver saw what was wrong, he grabbed a hammer and smashed the car window so the door could be opened and the baby set free. He was heralded as a hero by those watching—everyone but the mother. She was furious because he had broken the window. What was more important to her? The baby or the window?

We make hundreds of choices every day. Most choices have no right or wrong attached to them, like choosing what shoes to wear or whether to eat fish or chicken for dinner. But sometimes we face decisions that carry more weight.

Our day-to-day choices are very important. Living with their consequences and realizing their effect on other people should teach us to think and choose carefully. The wisdom to make right choices in small and large matters is a gift from God. Understanding this should make us more conscious of the decisions we make and more willing to include God in our decision making.

Ask God to give you a special awareness of just how important your choices are and a renewed commitment to make the right ones. Ask yourself, "What would Jesus do?" and "What would Jesus have me do?" and you will find direction to help you make the right choices.

GETTING FOCUSED

Begin your study by considering the following:

What are some possible criteria for making right choices?

BIBLE READING

1 Corinthians 10:23–33; 11:20–22; 16:13–14

New International Version

10:23 "Everything is permissible"—but not everything is beneficial. "Everything is permissible"—but not everything is constructive. 24 Nobody should seek his own good, but the good of others.

25 Eat anything sold in the meat market without raising questions of conscience, 26 for, "The earth is the Lord's, and everything in it."

27 If some unbeliever invites you to a meal and you want to go, eat whatever is put before you without raising questions of conscience. 28 But if anyone says to you, "This has been offered in sacrifice," then do not eat it, both for the sake of the man who told you and for conscience' sake—29 the other man's conscience, I mean, not yours. For why should my freedom be judged by another's conscience? 30 If I take part in the meal with thankfulness, why am I denounced because of something I thank God for?

31 So whether you eat or drink or whatever you do, do it all for the glory of God. 32 Do not cause anyone to stumble, whether Jews, Greeks or the church of God—

New Living Translation

10:23 You say, "I am allowed to do anything"—but not everything is helpful. You say, "I am allowed to do anything"—but not everything is beneficial. 24 Don't think only of your own good. Think of other Christians and what is best for them.

25 Here's what you should do. You may eat any meat that is sold in the marketplace. Don't ask whether or not it was offered to idols, and then your conscience won't be bothered. 26 For "the earth is the Lord's, and everything in it."

27 If someone who isn't a Christian asks you home for dinner, go ahead; accept the invitation if you want to. Eat whatever is offered to you and don't ask any questions about it. Your conscience should not be bothered by this. 28 But suppose someone warns you that this meat has been offered to an idol. Don't eat it, out of consideration for the conscience of the one who told you. 29 It might not be a matter of conscience for you, but it is for the other person.

Now, why should my freedom be limited by what someone else

New International Version

33 even as I try to please everybody in every way. For I am not seeking my own good but the good of many, so that they may be saved.

11:20 When you come together, it is not the Lord's Supper you eat, 21 for as you eat, each of you goes ahead without waiting for anybody else. One remains hungry, another gets drunk. 22 Don't you have homes to eat and drink in? Or do you despise the church of God and humiliate those who have nothing? What shall I say to you? Shall I praise you for this? Certainly not!

16:13 Be on your guard; stand firm in the faith; be men of courage; be strong. 14 Do everything in love.

New Living Translation

thinks? 30 If I can thank God for the food and enjoy it, why should I be condemned for eating it? 31 Whatever you eat or drink or whatever you do, you must do all for the glory of God. 32 Don't give offense to Jews or Gentiles or the church of God. 33 That is the plan I follow, too. I try to please everyone in everything I do. I don't just do what I like or what is best for me, but what is best for them so they may be saved.

11:20 It's not the Lord's Supper you are concerned about when you come together. 21 For I am told that some of you hurry to eat your own meal without sharing with others. As a result, some go hungry while others get drunk. 22 What? Is this really true? Don't you have your own homes for eating and drinking? Or do you really want to disgrace the church of God and shame the poor? What am I supposed to say about these things? Do you want me to praise you? Well, I certainly do not!

16:13 Be on guard. Stand true to what you believe. Be courageous. Be strong. 14 And everything you do must be done with love.

GAINING BIBLICAL INSIGHT
Exercising convictions with consideration

A common theme is woven through the previous seven lessons in this book. Like a golden thread through a patterned tapestry, it is always present without being stated. Regardless of the issue we confront, good decision making is essential to any solution.

The Holy Spirit helps us face life's difficult issues, but His presence does not automatically supersede our personal choices. We constantly encounter tough choices that shape us, decisions only we can make.

We can choose to accept Jesus and live for Him, or we can reject Him. We can choose to yield to the Spirit when He works in our lives, or we can ignore Him. We make financial choices and relationship choices. Ideally, we choose to live in a way that glorifies Christ in both our bodies and spirits.

Some choices are easy to make because the options are obvious. Others may be difficult because of possible ramifications. Paul gave guidelines to the Corinthians to help when making tough choices.

Choices Showing Consideration for Others as Individuals

If you were the only person living on the planet, choices would be easy because your decisions would affect no one but yourself. But we are not alone. Each of our actions is observed by others and may affect the choices they make. Paul taught the Corinthians the importance of considering the effect our actions can have on other people.

For example, Paul discussed a decision the Corinthians probably had to make daily—whether or not to eat meat that might have been previously offered as a sacrifice to idols. Paul gave guidelines in 1 Corinthians 10:23–33 for people faced with this decision. Notice the steps he took them through. The principles he taught apply to many daily decisions we make.

First, they had to decide for themselves whether eating the meat was right or wrong. What did he say about this and why?

What reasons did he give for them not to eat the meat at times, even if they felt it was all right for them to do so?

Note how Paul was teaching the Corinthians to consider other individuals when making decisions. Eating the meat (or some other action) might be permissible for individual believers, but he wanted them to consider what other people would think about their action. If others would be adversely affected, Paul told the Corinthians it would be better not to eat meat.

What motivated Paul to limit his own freedom of choice according to this passage?

Paul was driven by the desire to see people come to God. He did not seek his personal rights or pleasures but only what would influence others to be saved.

Choices Affecting the Common Good

Christian unity is inherent in Paul's teaching. He wanted Christians to be conscious of decisions and actions that affect not only other individuals but also the Church as a whole. Our choices should further the common good.

In 1 Corinthians 11:17–34, Paul discussed the observance of the Lord's Supper. He was disturbed by certain actions that were causing disunity among the believers.

In what way does participating in the Lord's Supper illustrate our unity in Christ?

What were the Corinthians doing that ignored or violated this unity?

Carelessly observing the Lord's Supper, without discerning the full meaning of the elements, led to actions that undermined the unity of believers. Paul urged the Corinthians to be perceptive about their actions and make choices that would benefit everyone.

What would be the results of ignoring Paul's admonitions? Of observing them?

Paul warned of the serious results of ignoring his instructions regarding the observance of the Lord's Supper. Likewise, Christians should seriously consider the effect our actions could have on Christian unity.

As poet John Donne wrote, "No man is an island." This is particularly true of Christians. We are each part of a great body of believers. Every choice we make reflects on the Body as a whole.

Choices Reflecting God's Love to Others

Paul encapsulated his teachings in a brief statement at the end of his letter (1 Corinthians 16:13,14). If we, like Paul, have a strong desire to see others come to Jesus, we should make choices that reflect God's love to everyone we meet.

To do this, we first must be very sure of what we believe, making sure we "stand firm in the faith." While we sometimes have options for making choices, matters of faith are settled. We do not budge on the foundational principles of our faith. The only choice we have is to stand firmly for what we believe.

Taking a strong stand for our faith takes courage, particularly if we face opposition. Paul recognized this requires spiritual strength. We count on the Holy Spirit to be our Helper, to give us the strength to stand courageously for our faith.

Paul reminded the Corinthians that firmness and boldness should not negate love. Everything (and the emphasis seems to be on that word) must be done in the love of God. Let the choices you make reveal the love of God in your life.

Eve was the first woman faced with choice. Unfortunately, she made a wrong decision. The entire human race has lived with the consequences of her action.

REFLECTING HIS IMAGE
Eve (Genesis 3)

Once, long ago, when time was not and the earth was dark and had no form—God created. "Through him all things were made; without him nothing was made that has been made" (John 1:3).

Sheltered by trees and flowers, Eve awoke to the sounds of a rushing waterfall and the distant humming of birds. It would be a day like every other, where time stretched out like a long, lazy, summer vacation.

She smiled and yawned as she greeted the morning and watched the sun rising, climbing high in the sky to provide needed warmth. She danced in the clear, clean waters and enjoyed the company of animals that had no fear of humans. Shameless as a baby, she, the first woman of all creation, literally fashioned by the hand and mind of God, stood poised and prepared to face a new day. She had it all—a beautiful place to live, the perfect diet, a flawless body, and a husband who adored her. Paradise—a perfect world.

"Now, at last, here is one who shares my identity—one to whom I can relate because she is everything I am, and I am everything she is. Here at last is another *person!*"[1] Adam had said when God brought Eve to him. "You are my equal in every way!" God had provided him with a partner, one who understood him. One who would help him. Adam would never be lonely again.

And so it began, at that very moment in time, the first pair clothed in innocence and love, hand in hand, began their walk in the cool of the evening—with God.

One beautiful day as Eve was walking in the Garden, tragedy struck. The serpent was sly, more sly than any wild animal God had made.

The serpent spoke to Eve. "Do I understand that God told you not to eat from any tree in the Garden?"[2]

"Oh no, not at all," Eve replied. "We can eat from any one of these trees. It's only that one, that one in the middle of the Garden that God said not to eat from. As a matter of fact, He said not even to touch it or we would die."

Superb in his evil strategy, the serpent continued. "You won't die. God knows that the moment you eat from that tree, you'll see what's really going on. You'll be just like God, knowing everything, ranging all the way from good to evil."[3]

What if this wise and lovely serpent is right? Eve wondered. *Suppose I am missing out on something. Can God be withholding something good?*

And then it happened. In an instant, she chose to disobey God. Her steps were measured as she made her way to the center of the Garden. A hush fell. *The tree looks good and think of what I will get out of it—knowledge. I will know everything! Imagine,* she reasoned. Slowly, methodically, she tasted the fruit and then offered some to Adam.

"What are you doing?" the beasts and birds must have asked. Those perfect inhabitants of the Garden who roamed freely with them every day had never seen such a strange and witless thing from Adam and Eve.

For as they watched—in that moment—sin entered their perfect world and this perfect woman who had it all, now realized she also had much to lose.

The first woman of all creation, literally fashioned by the hand and mind of God now stood naked, ashamed, her oneness with God and with her husband shattered. The serpent gloated.

And God said, "Yes. Yes, I know."

---

[1] Sue and Larry Richards, *Every Woman in the Bible* (Nashville: Thomas Nelson, 1999), 5.
[2] Genesis 3:1, *The Message.*
[3] Genesis 3:4,5, *The Message.*

EMBRACING THE PENTECOSTAL PERSPECTIVE
What is the Holy Spirit teaching me?

Eve made a bad choice; no one doubts it. She and every woman since have borne the lion's share of the guilt, singled out for her disobedient choice made with Adam at her side. Such are the consequences of bad decisions. They inevitably spread harm far and wide.

Sadly, we often do not realize or even consider the potential harm of our choices until we see the consequences. Believers have incredible powers of observation, but rarely exercise spiritual foresight when it comes to decisions of expedience or self-preservation. Can you imagine how many times Eve looked back and wished she had thrown the forbidden fruit at the serpent rather than eating it?

How can the fruit of the Spirit help in making wise decisions?

Is perpetual guilt a healthy state for a Christian? How can believers access the reality of forgiveness and move on?

How can prayer positively influence the outcomes of our choices?

Paul identifies himself most frequently as a "servant" or "slave" of Jesus Christ. It seems contradictory for Paul, who also wrote the Christian equivalents of great freedom documents (Romans and Galatians), to identify himself in this way. How, for example, can he expound on the agony of sin's bondage in Romans 7 and the glory of life in the Spirit in Romans 8 and then encourage purposeful suspension of Christian freedom in Romans 14? The answer is fairly simple. He understood the precarious distance traveled between death and life, and he was unwilling to become the pothole in another person's journey toward Christ.

How can we develop a greater sense of awareness of others' needs and keep from selfishly obeying our own desires?

Reflect on and discreetly share an example of a recent situation in which you yielded your own freedom for the sake of another's spiritual well-being.

Does God listen to the prayers of a night owl? Of course. Yet many a believer has been made to feel like a second-class disciple based on the timing of her devotional practice. And while the Word has much to say about rising early to pray, it does not specify a higher rate of return for such action. Prayer, the Bible clearly teaches, must be part of every healthy believer's life. The timing—including scheduled time and length—is a matter of conviction.

How can we know the difference between personal convictions and scriptural principles?

Why is it important to distinguish the difference?

How do personal convictions strengthen your daily walk?

INVITING GOD TO CHANGE MY VIEW
What change is God asking me to make?

Hurricane Katrina struck the Gulf Coast in 2005, carving a path of unimaginable destruction. Most of us will never forget the images of homes submerged in floodwaters or reduced to piles of kindling, the chaos of emergency response, and the ensuing crescendo of blame.

Long before the public officials' blame game had played itself out, individuals began to tell their stories of difficult choices made in the dark night of Katrina. Some were victims of circumstance, like the 911 operators in Mississippi who had to tell callers that they could not send help in the dangerous storm. Others were victims of their own poor choices, such as the medical student who confessed to leaving his assigned post at the Superdome when the crowd became frighteningly unruly. Though he later worked tirelessly to serve the medical needs of thousands, his guilt for his first choice could not be assuaged.

Jesus invited the disciples to stand at the headwaters of the end times and look ahead to the catastrophic events to come (Matthew 24). His teaching did not include details like dates or names, just an impending sense of the shortness of time, the approaching darkness, and the importance of carrying out His mission swiftly and powerfully. At this intersection of the present and eternity, people of the Spirit are called to live with integrity to the Word and the mission. Very few of the decisions we make each day do not affect that calling.

Have you asked forgiveness from God and other people you have hurt by your poor choices? Will you ask the Spirit to give you foresight into the consequences of your decisions? Do you need to focus on growing the fruit of the Spirit to temper your decision-making process? Will you follow the Spirit's lead when it means limiting your own freedom for the sake of the gospel?

Prayer

Father, I am thankful for the freedom You have given me in Christ. How wonderful to be free from the chains of sin and the darkness of a life apart from You! I understand You want others to experience this life. I do, too. As I live for You, give me the ability to do so with the heart of a servant. When this means laying aside my freedom for the sake of another, help me to do so without hesitation. While others contend for self-preservation, let me trust You as my Lord to let Your light shine through my service. In Jesus' name, Amen.

JOURNALING

Take a few minutes to record your personal insights from the lesson.

HOW TO LEAD A BIBLE STUDY GROUP

Welcome to the *Unlimited! . . . Bible Studies for Today's Pentecostal Woman* series! You will find these studies to be a great source for biblical guidance in living a Christian life in today's unsteady world and for learning more about the Holy Spirit's work in your life.

Leading a group in studying these lessons will be challenging and rewarding as together you discover how to apply God's Word to your life. You may have some questions about leading a Bible study. This section gives direction for answering the "why, who, what, where, when, and how" questions. Let's look at them individually.

"WHY" QUESTIONS
Why have a Bible study?

The first question you may ask is "Why do we want to have a Bible study?" This series is based on biblical, textual information, meant to be an expository study of what God's Word says on the topics presented in each lesson. Bill Bright, in his book *Discover the Book God Wrote*, says, "The Bible is so interconnected with God that we cannot separate it from His being. In fact, when we read the Bible with the right attitude, God, in the person of the Holy Spirit, joins with our spirit to help us understand it and apply it. The Book comes alive! The words in the Bible have life-changing power."[1]

Bible study group dynamics differ from other small group dynamics. Bible study is not necessarily easy, nor should those studying the Bible try to make it easy. Your main goal for beginning a Bible study

---

[1] Bill Bright, *Discover the Book God Wrote* (Wheaton, Ill.: Tyndale House, 2003), 5.

should not be for a group to have fellowship, although fellowship will occur. If your main purpose is something other than a direct study of God's Word to gain biblical understanding for each member's life today, you may want to consider a different curriculum and format. The main goal of Bible study is to understand the Bible in a more profound way, so it will penetrate deeply into the hearts of those attending.

Bible study differs from traditional small groups in that fellowship can happen before and after the study, but not necessarily during. The Bible study sessions may become intense at times while group members grapple with the life issues presented in these lessons. Lives will be changed as a result of understanding God's Word.

If you combine Bible study with the small group dynamics of worship, prayer, and fellowship, then take that into consideration when planning the length of time for your sessions. Be sure the Bible study time is not crowded out by other activities.

"WHO" QUESTIONS

Who are the study members?

Who are you going to invite to this study? Many possibilities exist for establishing a Bible study group: neighbors (presenting evangelism possibilities), a new converts' study, a working women's study, or an intergenerational study. Answering this question helps answer some of the other questions.

Determine if you are going to limit the size of the group and whether you are going to allow newcomers to this study once it has started. A recommended size would be no less than four and no more than eleven members. A study group of twelve or more should be divided into smaller groups to facilitate discussion.

Who is the leadership?

Another "who" question is answered by determining who makes up the leadership of this study group. Will more than one person be a facilitator (teacher)? Will you need others in leadership? For example, do you want a group secretary to keep information such as names, addresses, and e-mail addresses of group members in order to get information to each group member? Do you want a refreshment coordinator or special events coordinator if refreshments or fellowship events are to be a part of your time together? Who will these leaders be? These questions should be determined with the help of your church leadership. The women chosen for these positions need to be mature Christians.

"WHAT" QUESTIONS

The "what" questions will be partially answered when you answer the "who" questions. You may want to consider whether these sessions would be valuable for a Sunday School class, or adaptable to a couples' Bible study, in addition to the suggested women's study groups. Don't limit these studies to just one audience.

Also ask "What will be our format for each session?" These Bible study lessons offer a format that is workable for your study group; however, each group should adapt the lesson components to fit its needs.

"WHERE" QUESTIONS

Where to hold the Bible study meetings may be determined when you know who is coming. Many settings can be used for these studies, including a room at the church, a restaurant's private room, the lunchroom of an office, a community center, or someone's home. Once a location is determined, for maintaining the strength of the meetings, do not change locations.

"WHEN" QUESTIONS

When will you meet for Bible study? What day will you meet? How long will the meeting last? How long will it take to complete this book?

These studies are planned so that each lesson can be taught in one session, for a total of eight sessions. However, if your group wants to meet for a shorter amount of time each week, the lessons could be taught in two parts, for a total of thirteen to sixteen sessions. **One and one-half hours is a recommended time for each lesson** given in this series, assuming all lesson components are used in each session. Announce a planned start date and a final session date before beginning the unit of study.

The time of day for your meetings, of course, will be determined by the majority of the group attending, and the availability of the space you have chosen. You may want to build in time for fellowship before or after the Bible study; however, remember that it is better to have the study members wanting the meetings to be longer, rather than wishing they were shorter!

"HOW" QUESTIONS

How will you promote your Bible study sessions?

You may want to develop a brochure, place posters in the church hallways, ask for bulletin and pulpit announcements, or use any number of creative methods for getting information to potential group members. Be sure potential members understand how and where they can become involved in this study.

Carefully consider these questions and any others you may have to establish the framework for your Bible study. Trust God to be there as you meet with other women to discover how to apply His Word to your life.

TIPS FOR BEING A BIBLE STUDY GROUP MEMBER

Each Bible study group member is important to the success of these Bible studies. Use these suggestions to help make your time together more meaningful.

- Agree to participate: The more fully each person participates, the more each group member benefits. Agree to study the lesson before the scheduled session, and agree to attend the sessions consistently to share the insight God gives you about each lesson. During discussions, contribute actively without straying from the discussion or dominating the group's time together.
- Respect each other: Through open and honest sharing we encourage one another. We can talk about who we are—our hurts, hopes, joys, and struggles—and what God is doing in us in this study. Each group member has valuable contributions to make to these sessions and comments of each member should be honored.

- Keep a confidence: What is shared by other study group members during study sessions should stay as part of the group and should not be talked about outside study session time.
- Affirm each other: Affirmation strengthens the body of Christ. We can recognize what is best in other members of this study group and encourage them to develop these qualities as we grow spiritually together.
- Pray: Write down the prayer requests of other study members and pray for these requests during the week. Be aware that other study members will be praying for you.

Allow the Holy Spirit to work in your life through these Bible studies. God bless your time together with Him!

TIPS FOR BEING A BIBLE STUDY LEADER

As a leader, you have a determining role in the effectiveness of your Bible study group. Many resources are available to help you. Here are a few tips for some of your responsibilities as a group leader:

Demonstrate personal commitment to Jesus, the Word, and the people you lead.

As a leader, your personal commitment to God is of utmost importance. Leading a group of believers demands a strong personal commitment to God and His Word. Are you growing spiritually as an individual believer? Do you enjoy interacting with people? Do you want to see others grow spiritually? Then you will most likely be able to successfully lead a Bible study group.

Prepare thoroughly in prayer, study, and with a heart for the members of your group.

Use extra study helps if needed, such as Bible concordances, dictionaries, and study Bibles. Write notes in the margin of this study guide to help you facilitate discussion.

Decide before the first session if you will use every component offered in these lessons, or if you will choose only some of the components. See "Understanding and Using the Lesson Components" below for more information concerning each lesson segment.

The format for teaching these lessons will be interactive lecture and group reflection and discussion. Be so familiar with the lesson content beforehand that you will be able to keep the group moving forward in the lesson. Ask each study member to read the lesson and write out answers before coming to the session so they will also be ready for discussion.

Facilitate discussion. Know your group and the lesson well enough to carefully select key questions that will generate interaction; resist the temptation to lecture.

Keep the conversations biblically grounded by sticking to the topic of each lesson. Move on to the next question rather than allowing silence or "downtime," unless the silence is meaningful to the question being considered.

Guard a nurturing environment; encourage uplifting conversation, do not permit gossip, and insist on confidentiality. As much as possible, involve all study group members in the discussion at some time.

Always invite God's presence in your study sessions. Open and close each session with prayer, not as a formality but as a heartfelt necessity.

UNDERSTANDING AND USING THE LESSON COMPONENTS

You will find consistency in the components of each lesson in this book. An explanation of each component is given to clarify the purpose of each segment, enriching your total study experience.

CATCHING SIGHT
Introduction

The first component, "Catching Sight," directs the reader and study group to the topic of the lesson. Usually an anecdote or true-life story begins each lesson, followed by a brief explanation of the topic. Use these introductions to capture the attention of your group members as they are getting settled. If you are using this series for independent study, this introduction should help focus your mind as you begin.

GETTING FOCUSED
Begin your study by sharing thoughts on the following:

This component of the lesson initiates group discussion on the lesson topic. Break into groups of three to five to discuss the question or statement given in "Getting Focused." If you are studying independently, write down your thoughts on the question or statement. If you are leading a group, ask the group members to look at this question before the session and jot down some thoughts to facilitate discussion.

BIBLE READING

Bible passages selected to accompany each lesson are given in two versions: the New International Version and the *New Living Translation.* The two versions are side by side for easy reference during lesson study.

Shorter Bible readings may be read aloud by an individual or by the group. Longer readings should be read by group members before the session. Portions of the longer reading can be read during study time.

GAINING BIBLICAL INSIGHT

This component is the biblical exposition of the lesson. The pivotal truth of the lesson is given in italics beneath the component section heading. This is the "truth in a nutshell" concerning the topic of that lesson.

REFLECTING HIS IMAGE

This component gives an opportunity for creativity, as well as portraying the truth of the lesson. The Bible woman reflects the incarnation of the lesson's truths, and in most cases is given as an example of a life to emulate. This component can be used in several ways:

Individual devotional reading: Ask each group member to read this portion before coming to the study.

Small-group reading: Assign one person to read this component at the appropriate time in class or ask several women to read parts.

Drama: Assign women to portray each character in the Bible story and a narrator. Ask the women to give their practiced dramatic portrayal at an appropriate time in the study. Simple costumes will complete the effect.

Monologue: Request that one woman practice portraying the Bible woman in the lesson and present a dramatic monologue during the study.

EMBRACING THE PENTECOSTAL PERSPECTIVE
What is the Holy Spirit teaching me?

This perspective of a Pentecostal believer begins by asking, "What is the Holy Spirit teaching me?" We believe the Holy Spirit is a unique Person of the Trinity with a specific ministry in the life of a Christian. The questions raised in this component will help the Pentecostal believer apply the truths of the lesson in her own life.

INVITING GOD TO CHANGE MY VIEW
What change is God asking me to make?

After interacting with God's Word, seeing it in another woman's life, and discerning how it applies to one's own, there is one more essential step before we can live differently in light of the truth—prayer! This section provides questions that help each participant to go to the heart of the issue, asking God to bring change where it is most needed. Notice that there is usually a question provided to open the door for someone to receive Christ as Savior. A prayer is also included as a sample, a starting point, or simply as personal reflection.

JOURNALING
Take a few moments to record your personal insights from the lesson.

Space is given at the end of each lesson for writing down personal thoughts and reflections that transpire during the study of each lesson. The Bible study leader can take time for this in class or request that members complete this on their own time after the session.

AUTHORS

ARLENE ALLEN
—Catching Sight

The teacup collection that she keeps is a testament to the Southern hospitality one receives when meeting Arlene Allen. Born in the Appalachian mountains of Virginia, she never fails to delight and challenge her audiences with her quick wit and Southern-style wisdom.

An ordained minister with the Assemblies of God, Arlene is the director for the national Women's Ministries Department. She serves on the boards of the national Women in Ministry Task Force, Religious Alliance Against Pornography, and Global Pastors' Wives Network. She has an extensive speaking history that includes pulpit ministry, leadership training, and women's and ministers' wives retreats.

Arlene has been married for thirty-nine years to Gary R. Allen who serves as the executive coordinator of the Ministerial Enrichment office of the Assemblies of God. The Allens are parents of two sons and the proud grandparents of two "incredible" grandsons, Grant and Jacob.

PEGGY MUSGROVE
—Gaining Biblical Insight

In her book, *Musings of a Maraschino Cherry*, Peggy Musgrove talks about the role of a pastor's wife as sometimes like being the cherry on top of an ice cream sundae. But her life and ministry has been far more than just mere decoration.

Peggy is a speaker and freelance writer. Previously, she served as national director of Women's Ministries for the Assemblies of God and director of Women's Ministries for the Kansas District Assemblies of God. Peggy's written works include *Who's Who Among Bible Women, Pleasing God, Praying Always,* and articles for several publications. Peggy holds two bachelor of arts degrees, one from Wichita State University and one from Central Bible College.

Peggy and her husband, Derald, served in local churches and in district ministry in Kansas before moving in 1993 to Springfield, Missouri, where they both served in national offices for the Assemblies of God. They have two daughters, two "utterly awesome grandsons" and one "fabulously wonderful granddaughter."

When she's not writing, Peggy enjoys many things—reading, playing games, family holidays and vacations, spending time with her grandkids and friends, traveling with her husband, and antique shopping.

LORI O'DEA
—Embracing the Pentecostal Perspective & Inviting God to Change My View

With discipleship being the passion of her ministry, Lori serves as the doctor of ministry coordinator and visiting professor of practical theology for the Assemblies of God Theological Seminary (AGTS). Previously, Lori served on pastoral staffs in churches in Decatur, Illinois, and Waterford, Michigan.

Lori was born and raised in Michigan and spent eight years in Illinois before relocating to her current home in Springfield, Missouri. She shares her home with her awesome cat, named Zipper, who, she claims, can sail through the air like Michael Jordan. Aviation is one of her many interests and someday she would like to get her pilot's license. She's a firm believer that Mountain Dew, Doritos, and chocolate will be served in vast quantities at the Marriage Supper of the Lamb, though she has yet to find biblical support for her hopes.

Lori has spent a lot of time hitting the books and her educational credentials prove it. She earned a bachelor of science in missions and evangelism from Southwestern Assemblies of God University, and a master of divinity with a dual emphasis in biblical languages and pastoral ministry and a doctor of ministry in Pentecostal leadership from AGTS. In addition, Lori has served as a contributor to the *Complete Biblical Library* and *Enrichment Journal*.

CANDY TOLBERT
—Reflecting His Image

Candy Tolbert is a woman who "thinks out loud" about her love of God, love of spouse, love of children, and her passion for seeing others reach their full potential in Christ. A licensed minister with the Assemblies of God for twenty-six years, Candy is the national director of Missionettes ministries.

Her extensive background includes children's ministry, conference speaking, Christian education, missions, university student ministry, and music ministry. She has written articles appearing in the *Sunday School Counselor, SpiritLed Woman*, and *Leader's Touch* magazines and is co-author of the *Unlimited!...Bible Studies for Today's Pentecostal Woman*.

Candy has been married to her husband, Michael, for twenty-six years. Together they pastored several churches in the Southern California area. Candy is also the proud mom of two daughters, Rachel and Ashley. Candy's other passions in life include home decorating and good coffee.